W9-BND-011

RIDDLES IN HISTORY

Books by the Same Author

BEFORE COLUMBUS: Links Between the Old World and
    Ancient America

FORGOTTEN SCRIPTS: How They Were Deciphered and
    Their Impact on Contemporary Culture

HOMER AND BIBLE: The Origin and Character of
    East Mediterranean Literature

EVIDENCE FOR THE MINOAN LANGUAGE

UGARIT AND MINOAN CRETE

THE ANCIENT NEAR EAST

THE COMMON BACKGROUND OF GREEK
    AND HEBREW CIVILIZATIONS

UGARITIC TEXTBOOK

NEW HORIZONS IN OLD TESTAMENT LITERATURE

ADVENTURES IN THE NEAREST EAST

HAMMURAPI'S CODE: Quaint or Forward Looking?

SMITH COLLEGE TABLETS: 110 Cuneiform Texts Selected
    from the College Collection

LANDS OF THE CROSS AND CRESCENT

UGARITIC LITERATURE

THE LOVES AND WARS OF BAAL AND ANAT

RIDDLES IN HISTORY

BY CYRUS H. GORDON

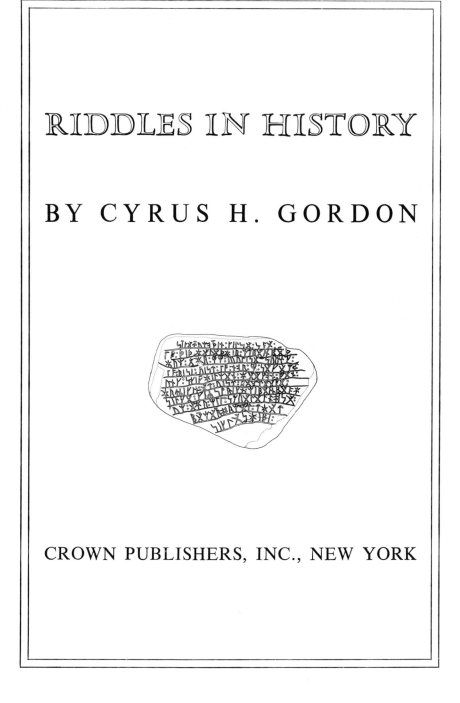

CROWN PUBLISHERS, INC., NEW YORK

The eight color plates (following page 30) depicting ancient ships are reproduced with the kind permission of Mr. Arie L. Ben-Eli, Director of the National Maritime Museum in Haifa, Israel.

Dedicated to

Alf Mongé

whose pioneer work in Old Norse cryptography
has opened up new vistas of history

CONTENTS

Contents

ERRATUM

The color section appears following page 62 instead of page 30 as indicated in the List of Illustrations and on the copyright page.

List of Illustrations

Maps

INTRODUCTION

This contribution to the history of trans-Atlantic crossings before Columbus, is evoked by a new dimension discovered in the inscriptions: cryptograms. But, as often happens when we investigate fresh avenues of approach, the implications go beyond what was envisaged. In fulfilling our specific goal, we have been brought to a major frontier in general cultural history.

Now and then an Egyptologist, Assyriologist, Hebraist, Hellenist, Latinist, or other expert, strays from the beaten path to call attention to cryptograms in his field. But the problem before us is international and affects the cultural history of our entire ecumene. To work with confidence in this area, it is not enough to be a specialist in one of the component fields, and to try to absorb at second hand the results of other specialists. This is not yet a subject for committees or computers. Instead it at this stage requires a personal control over all the essential elements—linguistic, epigraphical, cryptanalytic, and historical—from the original sources. Nothing on which conclusions are based in the following pages is at second hand.

Scholars are not expected to take anyone's word on faith. For their convenience, all the essential sources are between the covers of this volume. At the same time, I have tried to arrange the material so that the book will be as clear as possible to those who do not want to be excessively distracted by technicalities.

For typing my manuscript I am grateful to my former research assistant, Mrs. Edith Creter, who participated in the developments during 1968–71 that led to this book.

I owe thanks to family, friends, colleagues, students, publishers; my literary agent, Mrs. Carlton Cole; my editor, Dr. David McDowell; and Dr. John Lawrenz for the maps he prepared to illustrate this book.

I am especially beholden to my friends, Eugene and Emily Grant, whose encouragement at a difficult time made this book possible.

CHAPTER I

Stranger than Fiction

Moses Wilhelm Shapira committed suicide on 9 March 1884 in a small hotel in Rotterdam. His tragedy will help you understand this book.

In 1868 a German pastor, exploring the land of Moab east of the Dead Sea, chanced on a stone stela inscribed with ancient Canaanite letters. A young and scholarly French diplomat, Charles Clermont-Ganneau, and an English archaeologist, Captain Charles Warren, got wind of the discovery, went to the site (Dhiban, or biblical Dibon) and copied the inscription. The villagers then got the idea that the stone contained something of value beyond the text, so they proceeded to break the stela by repeatedly heating and cooling it. Most of the fragments were recovered and the stela may now be seen in the Louvre virtually restored to its original form, thanks to the copy made prior to the damage.

The text is of great interest for it gives the Moabite version of a ninth century B.C. war mentioned in the Bible (2 Kings 3:4 ff.). The stela is now called the Moabite, or Mesha, Stone after the Moabite King Mesha who records on it the withdrawal of Israel from Moab. According to Mesha, the Israelites were forced to retreat; according to the Bible, the withdrawal was voluntary.

13

War communiqués from opposing camps are as a rule slanted differently. In any case, the discovery of the stone proved the historicity of a biblical passage and was hailed sensationally throughout the world.

Antiquities dealers are in business to make money. Few of them care whether their wares are genuine or of recent manufacture. *Caveat emptor!* If an artifact is, regardless of age, worth its price to you, buy it. But don't pay fancy premiums for age, because even experts can be fooled by well-made fakes.

The discovery of the Mesha Stone touched off a spate of Moabite forgeries. Shapira, who happened to be an antiquities merchant in Jerusalem, was innocently taken in. He sponsored an excavation near Dhiban, which his Arab agents salted with manufactured pottery bearing Moabite inscriptions, that Shapira sold to the German Government. A German pastor named Weser had copied some of the inscriptions and convinced the German authorities that they were genuine. The German Government requested Shapira to obtain more at any price and not to sell them to anyone else.

Clermont-Ganneau exposed the forgeries, touching off a chain reaction that culminated in the Shapira tragedy. Once a person has scored a success, he may be inclined to try a repeat performance. Clermont-Ganneau, instead of sticking to positive discoveries, decided he would enhance his fame also by exposing fakes. He eventually got his chance.

Shapira was friendly with the sheikh of a tribe near Jerusalem, at whose home he heard an Arab tell an intriguing tale. The Arab was railing against natives who sell antiquities to foreigners. His indignation was not aroused by national pride, but because the possession of such relics brings good luck. To prove his point he recalled that some Arabs, fleeing from the Ottoman authorities, found refuge in caves around the Arnon Gorge, near Ara'ir. In the caves they found leather scrolls wrapped in cloth. Considering them worthless, they threw them away, but one of the Arabs had second thoughts. He retrieved and kept them, and was subsequently blessed with good fortune. His flocks increased and he became wealthy.

Shapira was struck by the fact that the texts had been found near Ara'ir (biblical Aroer), only a few miles east of Dhiban. He asked the sheikh to introduce him to the owner of the scrolls. A secret meeting was arranged and in four encounters, Shapira inexpensively obtained fifteen strips of parchment, which the owner said exhausted the collection.

The owner was, according to the sheikh, a rascal, and Shapira suspected he was furtive because he was wanted as a criminal. In any event, he disappeared without ever revealing his name or background to Shapira, and soon afterward the sheikh died. No one was left for checking Shapira's story.

Shapira was anxious to make a great discovery that would wipe out the stigma of the forgeries he had been duped into selling. He also craved wealth and fame. Though not a trained scholar, he knew Hebrew. He studied the parchments and found that they were a medley of Pentateuchal texts, mainly from Deuteronomy, albeit in the ancient Canaanite script. Since the earliest known copies of the Old Testament at that time came from about A.D., 900 he felt he had biblical manuscripts nearly two thousand years older, for the ancient letters were essentially those on the Mesha Stone of the ninth century B.C.

Shapira now sought scholarly support. Since he had connections in Germany, he turned to Dr. Konstantin Schlottmann, Professor of Old Testament at the University of Halle. This was ill advised because it was the Germans who through Shapira had got stuck with the Moabite forgeries, and Schlottmann had defended their authenticity, thus damaging his own academic reputation. This time Schlottmann was furious with Shapira and vehemently condemned the attempt to call a text that disagreed with standard Scripture a "biblical manuscript." Shapira, overwhelmed by the argument of the German savant, hid the parchments in the vault of a Jerusalem bank.

For some years Shapira applied himself to the normal operations of his antiquities shop, but he could not eradicate the scrolls from his memory. By chance he came upon a scholarly introduction to the Old Testament in which he read that the Pentateuch had been compiled from older documents, and that one of the documents (which we call "E" today) refers to God as "Elohim," whereas another of the documents (which we call "J") calls God "Jehovah" (actually "Yahweh" in the original Hebrew). Shapira remembered that his scrolls referred to "Elohim" even where the standard Hebrew text has "Yahweh."

Shapira's daughter Siona later wrote a biographical novel about her father, describing in detail his preoccupation with the scrolls after he had removed them from the vault for renewed study. She was very close to him and never doubted his integrity in the matter.

By May 1883, Shapira, convinced of his scrolls' authenticity, tried to sell them for a high price in Europe. In Berlin a committee of renowned experts met for an hour and a half and decided behind closed doors that they were fakes. They found what they considered conclusive evidence in a deviation from the wording in the standard Bible. The scroll read "Thou shalt not kill *the person of* thy brother." We now know that verbal deviations without altering the general sense, are quite normal in the copying of texts in antiquity.

Shapira was not informed of the committee's decision, but instead of waiting around in Berlin, he journeyed to London, where his scrolls were hailed in the press.

The decision as to whether the British Museum should buy the scrolls hinged on the verdict of an Old Testament textual expert, Christian David Ginsburg, who for three weeks worked intensively on the fragments, comparing them with the standard Hebrew text. *The Times* of London on August 10, 17, and 22 (1883) carried Ginsburg's translations. Everything looked rosy, for even Prime Minister Gladstone took time off from a busy schedule to see the fragments on display at the British Museum, and commented on their striking similarity to the script on the Mesha

Stone. But meanwhile, on August 15, an evil omen came across the English Channel in the person of Clermont-Ganneau. The latter promised Ginsburg he would not publish anything if only he would grant him the privilege of examining the texts. But Shapira refused to let his old enemy see the documents. Not to be outdone, Clermont-Ganneau had a look at two fragments on display in badly lit showcases in the British Museum, and on that basis claimed he was able to "prove" they were forgeries and to reconstruct exactly how they had been "fabricated." Clermont-Ganneau thereupon scooped Ginsburg by a day in a letter to *The Times*. Ginsburg, who had at least studied the texts, then presented his theory on how the forgery had been perpetrated. The academic establishment followed by the public jumped on the bandwagon, sealing the fate of Shapira who wrote the following letter on August 23 in a London hotel:

Dear Dr. Ginsburg!
   You have made a fool of me by publishing and exhibiting things which you believe to be false. I do not think I shall be able to survive this shame, although I am not yet convinced that the manuscript is a forgery. . . .
   I will leave London in a day or two for Berlin.
                                        Yours truly,
                                        M. W. Shapira

On 9 March 1884 Shapira shot himself after wandering around Europe as a tormented soul for half a year.
   In 1883 the verdict seemed so logical. How could leather and cloth survive for millennia in a country with an annual rainfall? How can you trust an antiquities dealer who obtained his wares from disreputable and ignorant natives? Who ever heard of Jewish manuscripts in the old Canaanite script? Since when did Jews hide manuscripts in caves? How gullible can one expect the scholars of Berlin, Paris, and London to be? But in 1947 something unbelievable happened just west of the Dead Sea.[1]

Hebrew scrolls were found in caves. They reached scholars through an antiquities dealer in Jerusalem, who got them from illiterate Bedouin. In fact the initial find was reported to have been made by a goat pursued by his unschooled shepherd—supposedly named Mohammed edh-Dhib, whom no one has since been able to locate. Cries of "forgery" were raised by many scholars. But the search was on and manuscripts up to two thousand years old were soon found in many caves west of the Dead Sea. We now know that the preservation of organic material in caves depends not so much on regional rainfall as on the natural formation of the particular cave.

The newly found Dead Sea Scrolls—like Shapira's—were found wrapped in cloth. Some of them were in whole or in part inscribed in the Old Canaanite script.

Excavations at Qumran (quite near the cave where the first scrolls were found in 1947), and the systematic and successful search for more scrolls in a number of caves by scientific teams, have established the authenticity of the Dead Sea Scrolls. The latter have also confirmed the genuineness of texts deviating from the standard Bible—not only verbally (where the sense is not usually affected)—but combining selections from different books of the Bible.

In brief, there is no longer any doubt that Shapira's parchments were genuine products of pre-Christian Jewish sectarians who hid their writings in caves east of the Dead Sea around the Arnon Gorge.

Professor Menahem Mansoor of the University of Wisconsin was the first to note that the Dead Sea Scrolls reopened the Shapira affair. And Dr. John Allegro has written a stirring book *The Shapira Affair* (Allegro, 1965).

The fate of the precious Shapira Scrolls is a warning to us not to let negators, no matter how great their reputations, perpetrate irreparable damage. The fragments, upon being branded as forgeries, lost their monetary value, were auctioned off for 25 pounds sterling as mementos of a hoax, and, being worth so little, have got lost. Since strangeness may indicate unusual value, apparent "fakes" should be catalogued and put in storage where they can be retrieved for future study if developments warrant it.

There are plenty of real fakes around. Antiquities dealers generally carry both authentic and forged antiques. They often know which is which, and if they like or respect you, will tell you the truth. It is not unusual for museum curators to purchase from dealers well-made fakes of known types, while rejecting genuine antiquities that deviate from what they are used to. In lands that once nurtured great civilizations, peasants are constantly plowing into tombs and other ancient constructions. Their marketable finds are acquired cheaply by dealers' agents. The most important finds of such origin are those with new features, though these are precisely the ones that are most liable to be branded as fakes by experts who are set in their ways and abhor change.

I have seen lots of fakes and even workshops in which they were being made. During World War II, I was called to the room of a Teheran hotel to evaluate some "important antiquities." There I found a cross-section of the antiquities underworld, who showed me two sculptures made from the same stone and cut with the same instruments, but 1500 years apart in style and subject matter. I told the ringleader they were fakes and he replied: "You are right but how do you know?" I explained that the ears of both pieces had been drilled by the same instrument so that the holes had the same bore, though the themes of the sculptures were a millennium and a half apart. He then informed me that his agents in New York have sold fakes to the best American museums, and all he wanted of me was to send the sculptures to his New York agents through the U.S. military mail to evade inspection. "But that is illegal," I protested. "No one will ever find out," he assured me. "But it is dishonest," I added. "We will never tell," retorted the rascal. "But this is unbecoming of an officer and gentleman," I gasped. "We understand exactly how you feel, Captain, and we are laying our cards on the table. We are prepared to make you a partner in the firm."

Some faked antiquities and inscriptions are so well executed that I do not profess to be able to differentiate them from the real thing. Conformity with the familiar makes forgeries very hard to detect. Drastic deviation from the norm is another matter. While at first it may be difficult to evaluate such artifacts, the passage of time gives us a means of checking, in fields where new discoveries and progress have been made in the interim. Forgers cannot anticipate future discoveries in a wealth of detail. The Shapira Scrolls illustrate this crucial principle.

The closing paragraphs of Allegro's book (p. 139) hit the nail on the head.

> ...the Shapira Deuteronomy opens a window on sectarian Judaism and early Christianity that the nineteenth-century critics all too precipitantly [sic] slammed shut again. At the same time, we should perhaps beware of too easily judging the motives of those scholars. It is more rewarding that we should learn from their mistakes and keep our minds open to possibilities and ideas that our present imperfect understanding cannot yet encompass. This is particularly so in the archaeological field, where almost every season brings fresh discoveries that demand a reassessment of outmoded theories and presumptions.
>
> If a reconsideration of the whole tragic affair of Shapira's manuscript has induced us to examine afresh the motives underlying our own scholarship, and thrown even a little new light on our own cultural heritage, Moses Wilhelm Shapira will not have died in vain.

We have recounted the Shapira affair because it is typical. The reader who grasps its significance will be able to discriminate between evidence and opinion, and to know why there is often such a gap between them in the topics under discussion.

No politically astute member of the establishment who prizes his professional reputation is likely to risk his good name for the sake of a truth that his peers (and therefore the public) may not be prepared to accept for fifty or a hundred years. A Persian anecdote is a propos.

A vizier once remarked to the Shah that in a certain province in India, the grain grew as high as an elephant's ear. The Shah, who disliked exaggeration, warned the vizier: "Never indulge in such loose talk again, if you want your head to remain attached to your body." The terrified vizier held his peace until fifteen years later, while accompanying the Shah on a campaign in that very province in India. There he called His Majesty's attention to the gigantic grain which was indeed as high as an elephant's ear: "You see, O King of Kings, I spoke the truth!" "Let this be a lesson to you," retorted the Shah, "never make statements that take fifteen years to prove."

In describing other genuine but challenged discoveries, we shall observe that proof of their authenticity never depends on affidavits or the trustworthiness of witnesses. The folly of judging such issues by the character of the dramatis personae is brought out by a famous Arab yarn. A respected Muslim gentleman was caught drinking wine, which is forbidden to true believers in this world, and permitted only in paradise. The Muslim extricated himself by explaining: "The fluid I am drinking was brought to me by my Christian servant who bought it as wine from a Jewish merchant. How can true believers accept the testimony of a Christian who cites a Jew as his authority?"

When bona fide archaeologists have found an inscription in situ in a professionally conducted excavation, we shall trust their official scientific report. Otherwise we shall attach no weight to the circumstances of discovery, any more than we have attached weight to the testimony of Shapira who got the scrolls from an unnamed rogue. The *internal* evidence in the light of *subsequent* discovery provides the proof of authenticity, when the disputed material is full of unprecedented peculiarities that *later* turn out to be genuine.

We shall narrate how the inscriptions of importance for this book came to light, because the human side of the story is full of interest per se and, like the Shapira tragedy, may help us preserve an open mind when similar situations arise in the future.

On 11 September 1872 someone mailed the following letter to
Viscount Sapucahy, president of the Instituto Historico in Rio de
Janeiro.

Mr. Viscount,
    As I was having stones moved on my property of Pouso Alto near
the Paraiba, my slaves brought me one which they had already
broken into four pieces. That stone bore numerous characters which
no one understood. I had them copied by my son who knows a bit of
draughtsmanship, and I decided to send this copy to Your Excellency, as President of the Historic and Geographic Institute of Brazil, to
see whether Your Excellency or someone else can find out what these
letters mean. Since I have come to the capital and have not the time
to deliver them personally to Your Excellency, I am mailing them to
him.
    I am with complete consideration and respect
                                        Your Excellency's
                               Attentive, devoted and obliged servant
                                        Joaquim Alves da Costa
Rio, 11 September 1872

Brazil in 1872 was on the fringes of European culture with very
limited intellectual resources in esoterica like ancient scripts. The
Emperor, Dom Pedro II (1825–91), had an amateur's love for
Near Eastern studies, especially Hebrew and Arabic, but what he
knew fell far short of professional expertise. Outside of the Emperor no one in Brazil had even a reputation for adequate knowledge in such matters. So the Viscount entrusted the study and
publication of the text to a bright and well-traveled naturalist,
Dr. Ladislau Netto (1838–94), Director of the Museu Nacional
in Rio. Netto identified the script as "Phoenician" and plunged
into the study of Hebrew and of what little was then known of
Phoenician with the intensity of a spirited pioneer. Netto soon
surmised the significance of the text: it recorded an ancient sailing from the Red Sea port of Ezion-geber to Brazil. As a naturalist, he showed how the winds and currents facilitate crossings
from the bulge of Africa to the bulge of Brazil. But it is one thing

to be intelligent and perceptive, and quite another to master the ins and outs of an atypical Canaanite inscription. Matters were not helped by the fact that neither "Joaquim Alves da Costa" nor the plantation at Pouso Alto has been located. There are many Pouso Altos in Brazil, and in 1872 there were still more; also there are two widely separated Paraibas: the Province of Paraiba up north near the bulge, and the Region of the Paraiba River down south around the latitudes of Rio and São Paulo.

Quite possibly "Joaquim Alves da Costa" is a pseudonym. Perhaps the finder wanted a free and publicized professional evaluation of the text to enhance its price. But there is another possibility.

In 1873 Netto published his view that the Paraiba inscription might well be authentic and bear witness to a trans-Atlantic crossing in the sixth century B.C. The editor of the newspaper *Jornal de Comercio* felt obliged to cast doubt on the text. Nevertheless, the sensational article by Netto was picked up by the press all over the world, so that it could not be disregarded by the experts.

The famed head of the international establishment in such matters was Ernest Renan (1823–92) of Paris, with whom the Emperor and Netto corresponded. Netto did not entrust the whole text to Renan but sent him only excerpts so that the French savant could help, but not scoop him. Renan replied that while no one can really pass judgment on an inscription he has not personally examined, he was nonetheless confident it was a forgery. (It takes a "great" man to get away with such inconsistency.) It is interesting to note that Renan based some of his arguments on his misreadings of the text. As an intellectually insecure amateur in Brazil, the Emperor accepted Renan's verdict. Without Dom Pedro's support, Netto was doomed to ignominious failure even on his home front, for he lacked the knowledge to stand up to Renan in Canaanite linguistics and epigraphy.

Then, as later in the Shapira affair, there were competent

scholars who opted for authenticity. The most rational and constructive expert was Professor Konstantin Schlottmann, whom we have already mentioned. In 1874 he published a serious scientific article showing that while some elements looked suspicious, others inspired confidence in the authenticity of the Paraiba inscription. In sum, he advocated openmindedness in the matter, for which he reaped a harvest of abuse from his peers. He was hit particularly hard by Professor Mark Lidzbarski whose dogmatic arguments for "forgery" are now contradicted by discoveries of the twentieth century. Thereafter the Paraiba inscription (like the Shapira scolls) remained officially a "forgery" which no scholar could reconsider with impunity.

The intellectuals of Rio—like all such circles in any city—were gossipy and cruel. Netto became the butt of ridicule, which was unbearable to a man of station and merit who cherished his reputation.

By 31 January 1874 (the date of the letter translated below from the original French), he had begun to have serious doubts about the text, though he still hoped that more evidence would turn up to prove its authenticity. He then sent the following letter to Wilberforce Eames (1855–1937) of New York City, with a carefully prepared facsimile of the master copy of the inscription.

31 January 1874

My dear Sir:

It is only now that I am able to answer the letter by which you honored me in writing during July of last year. Before writing to you I tried to get some positive data for you about the Phoenician monument which I know only from the copy of which I am sending you the attached facsimile with translations into Hebrew and French regardless of the inaccuracies in them. Unfortunately, in spite of the official and private steps which I have taken to locate the person who sent us the copy of the monument, I have no news of him. If it is a ruse, I cannot detect what prompted it, for nearly two years have passed since that manuscript was sent to the Historical Institute of Brazil, and up to now, nobody has claimed to be its author. Further-

FACSIMILE OF THE PARAIBA INSCRIPTION
A tracing of Netto's facsimile made from the master copy of the inscription. This facsimile was mailed from Rio de Janeiro to New York on January 31, 1874.

more, the dispatch was made under such natural circumstances that no one suspected a mystery.

Accept, Sir, the assurance of my most respectful sentiments.

Ladislau Netto
Director of the National Museum

The torments that Netto suffered during the next decade can only be surmised from the fact that he brooded all that while until he mustered enough courage to publish a retraction entitled *Lettre à Monsieur Ernest Renan* (Netto 1885).

In this booklet dated 1885, Netto confesses that ten years earlier, in 1875, he concluded through the following ruse that the text was a forgery. He made a list of all the people in Brazil in 1872 who had enough knowledge to compose such a text. The list had only five names: one native of Brazil and four foreigners. The native (Dom Pedro II ?), whom he knew well, was in Netto's opinion not guilty so he struck him off the list. Netto then wrote to all four foreigners letters that called for a reply. One of the answers was, in Netto's judgment, in the handwriting of the 1872 letter signed "Joaquim Alves da Costa." To make sure there was no mistake, Netto wrote another letter to the suspect, and the handwriting confirmed his suspicion. However, the "villain's" social prominence and reputation for scholarship and integrity prevented Netto from divulging his name.

Graphology is tricky business, and all of us learned in 1971–72 from the Clifford Irving affair that even professionals make mistakes. Netto was no graphologist, nor does his failure to name the guilty party inspire confidence. In no case are we going to base conclusions on Netto's graphology or veracity, though my investigations inspire confidence in Netto's intelligence and character. But let us suppose that Netto did indeed identify the guilty party by his handwriting, and that the culprit was in fact erudite, reputable, and prominent. That kind of worldly man (especially during the appearance and exposure of Moabite fakes that followed the 1868 discovery of the Mesha Stone) would not be inclined to risk disgrace when through a trick he could see how the Establishment would react. If the reaction was favorable, he could come forward triumphantly with the Stone; and if world scholarship condemned it as a fake, he could lie low and not bother with a worthless object that could only bring him trouble and shame.

The Netto and Shapira affairs unfolded during the same era (1868–85). Schlottmann, who had got the bastinado for his openmindedness regarding the Paraiba Stone, had little stomach for further martyrdom through openmindedness with the Shapira scrolls. Moreover, the great Renan who emerged victorious in branding the Paraiba Stone a forgery, was the professor of Clermont-Ganneau, who duplicated his master's triumph by declaring the Shapira scrolls a fake. There is no doubt about it. A big shot at the Louvre or Collège de France, though factually wrong, will impress the world more than a Jerusalem shopkeeper or even a Brazilian museum director, though right.

Part of the problem was, of course, that neither Shapira nor Netto had the professional training to hold his own with renowned scholars like Renan, Clermont-Ganneau, or Ginsburg. Shapira, who was accused of forgery and not merely of being duped, blew his brains out; Netto, whose judgment (but not as a rule his character) was assailed, lost faith in his discovery, suffered public ridicule for a decade, "confessed his error" in abject subservience to the Establishment headed by Renan, and lived out the rest of his shortened life with indelible memories of his humiliation.

The Paraiba Affair is far from over.[2] I became involved when Professor Jules Piccus of the University of Massachusetts at Amherst sent me, in November, 1967, the hitherto unpublished facsimile of the text with Netto's letter of 31 January 1874. I knew the text was generally regarded as a fraud, and therefore examined it critically in the light of what scholars had written about it, and especially of the evidence discovered after 1872. In 1968 I announced my reasons for considering it genuine,[3] not realizing that 1968 was being celebrated in Brazil as the five-hundredth anniversary of the birth of Pedro Alvares Cabral, the Portuguese navigator who discovered Brazil in 1500. Cabral was on his way from Portugal to India via the Cape of Good Hope. As a good sailor, he kept a safe distance from the African shore where the bulges of Africa and Brazil are separated by the narrowest part of the Atlantic Ocean. Against his plans, the winds and currents brought him to Brazil. He remains the heroic Portuguese discoverer of Brazil. What Columbus means emotionally to the American Italians, Cabral means to the nationalists of Brazil.

My announcement concerning the Paraiba text evoked immoderate attacks from certain members of the Brazilian establishment, for I had innocently undermined Cabral's priority and "Portuguese honor." The treatment I have received at the hands of Brazilian individuals has been generally cordial, especially from those who believe in an ancient Phoenician presence in Brazil. But the blasts I got in the press were on occasion beyond reason as well as taste. The fact that the Brazilian academies lack competence in Canaanite linguistics and epigraphy makes its university prima donnas who rank as authorities on Brazilian history (from the beginning of time!) particularly vicious.

Brazilian friends arranged an appearance for me on the leading Rio television program for interviewing authors and celebrities. It was announced, like all the TV programs, in the newspapers. A nationalist historian had just attacked me in the press. The TV program opened, and it was announced that I would presently be interviewed on an ancient inscription of great interest in Brazilian history. Then suddenly, before my interview could begin, the power was cut off. In a few minutes, we were informed that the program of the evening was canceled (not merely rescheduled). Was it an accidental power failure? Maybe. But many of my Brazilian friends did not think so.

The Paraiba Affair still continues to haunt Brazil. The official view is that the *Lettre à Monsieur Renan* has closed the matter (e.g., Junior 1970). A Brazilian gentleman, Nicolau Duarte Silva (Silva 1972), while subscribing to the "forgery" view, most decorously exculpates me from the suspicion of malice toward the memory of Cabral. On 18 November 1969 I wrote him a letter which he cites on the cover, on the title page, and in the article (p. 192) in English and in Portuguese translation: "My work on the Brazil inscription is based entirely on the fact that it is full of grammatical, lexical and stylistic forms which were unknown in 1872 and which have since appeared in excavated inscriptions. When I announced my findings in 1968 I was totally ignorant that it was an important anniversary of Pedro Cabral."

How easy it is to misunderstand others! In 1968 Brazilians in high places considered me a Gringo motivated by a desire to strip Cabral of his glory. I have worked as a Semitist—not as a North American chauvinist—and it was only after my 1968 announcement that I paid any attention to Cabral and his achievements.

Shapira ended his misery with a bullet. Netto lived out his chagrin, which was fortunately counterbalanced by professional advancement. Though the two men were very different, they paid a high price for announcing the truth about important inscriptions in old Canaanite letters, nearly a century before the truth was demonstrable through *subsequent* discoveries.

Both the Shapira and Netto texts are known only from copies. The original Shapira scrolls were seen by reputable witnesses (Ginsburg, Clermont-Ganneau, and other German, French, and British scholars). No identified witness has seen the original Paraiba Stone. There is a chance the Shapira scrolls will reemerge, because they were bought at a London auction. If the Paraiba Stela is someday located, being stone it may be found in a better state of preservation than the leather scrolls of Shapira.

The next discoverer in our story was of an entirely different type. Unlike Shapira, who could read a number of languages, and quite unlike Netto, who was highly educated and prominent, Olof Ohman was a barely literate farmer who had migrated to Minnesota from a remote part of northern Sweden where he received only nine months of schooling. Being naturally intelligent, Ohman learned to read, but he never could write a letter without help. In his village of Kensington, Douglas County, Minnesota, Ohman obtained a tract of land for farming that needed to be cleared of trees. In November 1898 he was removing an aspen tree, about eight inches thick, breast high. Dendrologists have calculated that in that climate it takes an aspen tree of that size about sixty-nine years to grow. The tree therefore would have started its life around 1829, long before there were any post-Columbian white inhabitants in that region.

Ohman was strong. His method of removing the tree was to cut through the lateral roots by digging a circular trench, and then, using the tree itself as a lever, pulled it out to one side, vertical roots and all. Enmeshed in its vertical roots was a stela on which Ohman's son noticed writing. The monument, now known as the Kensington Stone, contains a runic inscription in Norse, commemorating an expedition of Scandinavians who reached that area in A.D. 1362 from Vinland.[4]

Ohman's discovery was in full view of a neighbor's house. Anyone who has lived in a village knows that there are no secrets. Those who deny the authenticity of the Kensington Stone say that Ohman (or an accomplice) forged it, or that he somehow slipped it under the roots of the aspen, or that the testimony is unreliable, etc.[5] Unlike the Shapira Scrolls or the Paraiba Stone, the Kensington Stela is preserved (in the museum at Alexandria, the county seat of Douglas County, Minnesota).

The preservation of the actual monument makes no difference to the negators who refuse to accept the testimony of an ignorant farmer, when "science requires professional archaeological excavation." As we shall see later, the negators do not like the unwelcome Bat Creek Stone, which has been professionally excavated, published, and preserved by a prestigious archaeological institution. Our conclusions must rest not on taking sides in the controversy regarding Ohman's character and the reliability of his account of the discovery, but solely on the internal evidence of the text, in the light of new discoveries and developments since 1898, for much has meanwhile happened in runic and related studies.

The first Nordic specialists who studied the Kensington Stone succeeded in reading VINLAND but not the pentathic numerals of the date 1362 (A.D.). For them VINLAND implied the age of Leif Erikson who reached America around A.D. 1003. The runologists soon noted forms in the Kensington Stone that are too late for the eleventh century, and therefore they concluded the Stone was a forgery. The finger was most often pointed at Ohman, though since he could hardly write Swedish or English, some preferred to accuse Sven Fogelblad, a clergyman who had been ruined by drink. It was at first assumed that Fogelblad had studied runology as part of his theological training in Sweden. The fact that theological education in Sweden made no place for runology was

1

2

THE KENSINGTON STELA

The two inscribed surfaces of the Stela: (1) the obverse, and (2) the left side. This Stela is now on display in the Museum at Alexandria, the Douglas County seat, Minnesota.

not permitted to spoil the amateur detective work.

Like most unschooled people, Ohman and his fellow villagers held university professors in awe. If the greatest scholars on the campuses of Scandinavia and America said the Stone was a forgery, then a forgery it must be. What perplexed the Kensington farmers was how there could be a forgery without a forger, and how did the Stone get under the tree.

Unlike Shapira who sought fortune and fame, and unlike Netto who had intellectual stature, Ohman was a barely literate farmer who expected no wealth beyond his crops, and no attention outside his community. He certainly had no academic position to maintain, to enhance, or to risk. Yet he had a sense of personal worth and he prized his good name. Nobody—least of all a nineteenth-century Swedish peasant—wanted to be known as a forger. The notoriety, at home and abroad, which made him out to be a fraud, was anathema to him. To get the source of his chagrin out of sight, he dumped the Stone (luckily face down) on his barn floor, and tried to forget his ill-fated discovery.

That is the way things remained until 1907, when a young scholar, Hjalmar Rued Holand, visited Kensington while gathering material for a book on the Scandinavian communities of America. The Kensington folk were still talking about the Stone, which after all is still the hamlet's only claim to fame. Holand called on Ohman and the encounter had two results: (1) it kindled Holand's interest in the Stone, and (2) Ohman got rid of the unpleasant inscription by presenting it as a gift to Holand.

After a few years had passed, Holand began to study the Stela. It was he who first succeeded in translating the whole text including the numerals "1362." He took on the opposition gallantly, for which he is still hated *post mortem* by the negators. He was not, as his enemies still imply, a rank amateur. When the Stela was found in 1898, he was already working on his M.A. thesis "The Age and Home of the Elder Edda" at the University of Wisconsin. Obviously such a disturber of the pax academica is not welcome on the campus as a faculty member, and he did not have a career in the university system. But for half a century he stood up against the professional runologists and slugged it out point by point, showing that the condemnation of the text had been based on a false chronology that was three and a half centuries too early, and that the peculiarities of the text were matched in other fourteenth-century texts.[6] In his battle, he was not completely alone, for in addition to some popular support (which in fact has little validity in technical matters), a few fully qualified runologists brought to light proofs that the suspected errors in the Kensington Stone are indeed correct.[7]

In April 1972 my wife, Joan, and I visited Alexandria with our friend, Professor Don Lawrence of the University of Minnesota. At the Museum there, we examined the Stela which is well preserved. Joan observed that the base of the Stela tapers, suggesting that it was hewn to fit into a socket. Moreover, the text is continued not on the reverse, but on the left side, which indicates that the back was not visible but against a wall, when it was installed upright in its intended position. Through the mediation of Dr. Lawrence, the Ohman farm in Kensington is being searched for the socket into which the Stela fitted, and under the initiative of the Mayor of Kensington, funds are being sought for purchasing the Ohman farm as an archaeological preserve.

My involvement with the Kensington Stone took over four decades to incubate. As an undergraduate at the University of Pennsylvania I studied Swedish and Dano-Norwegian under Professor Axel Johann Uppvall. His infectious love of the Scandinavian languages made an indelible impression on me. He once told me: "If you have not studied Old Icelandic, you have missed half of life right there." While I do not take such statements literally, his words never stopped haunting me. This by way of explaining my long involvement—academic and sentimental—with Scandinavian languages including Old Norse. Through the local Swedish Society in my native city of Philadelphia, I made contacts with the American-Scandinavian Foundation which in 1939 sent me to Uppsala, Sweden, as a Fellow.

In the 1920s and 1930s, it was too much of a historic leap to
reckon with Norsemen in pre-Columbian Minnesota. In those
days any talk of Vikings even in Vinland was far out. So without
looking into the Kensington Stone itself, I simply accepted the
consensus of opinion—shared by my beloved teacher and the
whole establishment—that as a known fake, the Kensington
Stone was worthless.

The strongest opposition to the Kensington Stone stems not
from Columbus-proud Italians, but from runologists of Scandinavian background who subconsciously recoil from anything
that might be construed as ethnocentrism. This is illustrated by
the ethnic background of Wahlgren and Blegen who have written the most widely cited books against the authenticity of the
Kensington Stone.

In the controversy, both sides have stooped to name-calling
and vilification. Further deterioration can be expected as the new
evidence for authenticity assails the consensus of runological
opinion.

My involvement with the Kensington Stone started in 1968
after the wide publicity given to my reevaluation of the Paraiba
Stone. People from all over the world brought to my attention
various American inscriptions thought to be in pre-Columbian
Old World scripts. A Norwegian amateur questioned me about
the Kensington Stone. After securing good photographs from the
Smithsonian Institution in Washington, D.C., I began to interpret the text. Gradually I got into the secondary literature and
started to correspond with a number of qualified runologists in
Norway who are endowed with independent minds. They showed
me that the supposed "errors" in the Stone were authenticated in
fourteenth-century Nordic texts.

In mid-June 1971, Dr. O. G. Landsverk, the crusader in the
cause of authenticating the American runestones, unexpectedly
called on me, to convince me of the genuineness of the Kensington Stone by explaining the new dimension of the problem: the
runic cryptograms solved by Mr. Alf Mongé. This aspect of the

problem was quite novel to me, and I asked some technical questions which Landsverk mistook for disbelief. I assured him I was already convinced of the Stone's authenticity, though I might require a little time to follow the ins and outs of certain cryptograms. Landsverk is so accustomed to running into hostility among academicians, that he was quite unprepared to meet one already on his side. He and his gracious wife gave me two books that embraced Mongé's solutions of many runic cryptograms.[8]

I have never met Alf Mongé personally, but since June 1971 we have become close friends through correspondence. My training has not predisposed me to take on faith things I do not understand. A word is needed to explain why I was able to evaluate Mongé's work positively in a matter of days. Cryptography can be tricky; cryptanalysis is exceedingly technical. Mongé has made a lifework of cryptanalysis, whereas I am a professional philologian. However, he and I have enough common background to enable us to communicate with each other in a field that is closed to most scholars. During World War II we were both cryptanalysts in the U.S. Army Signal Corps. We got our experience cracking enemy codes and ciphers. Our mentor was the late William Friedman, who created the world's greatest cryptanalytic center and who trained a cadre of outstanding disciples, who in turn trained Mongé and me among many others. Friedman's home study courses in cryptanalysis provided both of us with methodical and graded training in cryptanalysis, which we applied on the job during the working day. Some of our outfit's record of achievement has been declassified and published.[9]

Philologians who cannot follow the solutions of cryptograms in the inscriptions they seek to interpret, are not to be blamed. No man of science should be asked to believe or endorse what he cannot understand. At the same time, Mongé and I are not to be blamed for understanding ancient and medieval cryptograms. Everybody has strengths and weaknesses, areas of competence and gaping voids. All that is expected is that we evaluate ourselves and others realistically. Mongé, encouraged by Landsverk, has authenticated the Kensington Stone by solving its cryptograms of types that had been forgotten for centuries. More than that, he has raised runology to a new level and demonstrated the genuineness of the Spirit Pond Runestones, whose story we are about to tell.

The final episode of discovery told in this book took place quite recently. On 27 May 1971, Mr. Walter J. Elliott, Jr., who works as a carpenter in Quincy, Massachusetts, was visiting an aunt in Bath, Maine, where he was born on 16 March 1928. Pursuing his hobby of looking for old artifacts, he chanced upon three runestones at Spirit Pond, near Popham Beach, Maine.

His formal education ended in his sophomore year at high school. Then, after serving for five years with the Merchant Marine, he was drafted into the Army in 1948. A year later he was discharged only to be recalled by the Army for three years service in the Korean War, including seven months of combat duty. On regaining his civilian status, he went to work as a carpenter in Colorado. His marriage there ended in divorce. Then, after working in Florida and South Carolina, he returned to New England where he has been plying his trade of carpentry. He likes navigation and once tried to sail his boat solo across the Atlantic, but the voyage ended at Nova Scotia because of rudder trouble. For his efforts he won the stipulated consolation award for an unsuccessful try. Though quiet and reserved, he has an adventuresome spirit and a lively intelligence unspoiled by too much schooling.

He owns a magnetometer which he uses for locating metallic treasure. On one occasion he discovered a hoard of nineteenth-century U.S. coins buried at the residence of an old Maine recluse who had died. He often seeks arrowheads and other Indian relics.

On 27 May 1971 Elliott decided to look for artifacts on the secluded west bank of Spirit Pond. In his rubber raft he rowed over to it, after parking his car on Highway 208.

The tides there are so high that their rise and fall are eroding the bank. Elliott noted an eroding spot where a stone had been partly exposed. He picked it up and on cleaning off some dirt and moss, found carvings on it. That stone (now called SP-3) bears the longest of the Spirit Pond inscriptions. Elliott's natural curiosity led him back to the spot a few minutes later to look for more; he did so and found the two other Spirit Pond runestones: first SP-1 (with a map of the area) and then SP-2.

Elliott took the stones to the Bath Marine Museum, where the curator, Mr. Harold E. Brown (a retired high school teacher of mathematics), correctly identified them as runestones. Elliott then tried in vain to find an archaeologist at Bowdoin College in nearby Brunswick, Maine, but instead met a local journalist who published the story with photographs in the *Bath-Brunswick Times Record* (vol. 5, no. 111) on 8 June 1971. The article brought the discovery to the attention of the local public, including officials. The news also reached Mr. Richard Card while visiting Brown at the Museum in Bath. Card is a native of Bath whose elderly father lives there in the family home. Card, though now residing and working in Boston, visits Bath fairly often to see his father. Sensing the importance of the discovery, Richard Card got in touch with Elliott whom he had not known previously.

Richard Card is a graduate of Bowdoin College, where he made a distinguished record including election to Phi Beta Kappa in his junior year. Rightly assessing the significance of Elliott's find, he decided to play the role of intermediary so that the best authorities should bring their knowledge to bear, and counterbalance the necessary but unqualified enthusiasm of the amateurs.

In such matters the constructive function of the amateurs is to call public attention to potentially important discoveries that specialized scholars shy away from because of the professional hazards. An amateur, unencumbered by much knowledge, with no reputation at stake, can champion an unconventional cause with nothing to lose, and a lot of excitement to gain. Let us make

SP-! obverse (the map)

SP-1 reverse

SP-2

SP-3 obverse

SP-3 reverse

THE SPIRIT POND RUNESTONES
(Courtesy of Mr. Richard Card)

no mistake about it: runology is not milk for sucking babes, and the epigraphical and philological analyses of amateurs are of little or no value. The modicum of their wheat is generally buried in the huge stack of their chaff. But if the professionals have a monopoly of such source material, they will normally bury it by doing absolutely nothing. Their reasons are quite understandable. Inscriptions such as the Spirit Pond Stones are bound to be controversial for a long time. Scholars with established reputations and positions shun controversy because, regardless of which side they take, they will be attacked and abused by other members of the Establishment. But once the amateurs and journalists have announced a controversial discovery, the scholars are forced (albeit reluctantly) to take a stand. As the respected authorities in their field they cannot indefinitely say "I don't know," for such a confession implies incompetence. This puts them in a most unenviable position. If escape through silence is impossible, the easiest course is to brand the new material as a hoax and thus rule it out of court as invalid. This assures the consensus of their peers, usually for the duration of their life. Solid citizens, in academia as elsewhere, are not expected to rock the boat.

Card launched the subject effectively, by making the material, including his own photographs, available to scholars, amateurs, and journalists alike.

Meanwhile, Elliott, having exhausted the limited runological expertise in Maine, did what he could to find out who the real experts were. He unfortunately met with complete indifference at the Peabody Museum in Cambridge: a searing introduction to the strongholds of archaeological competence. He scrutinized the resources in the Public Library in Quincy, Massachusetts, the town in which he works as a carpenter. With the help of an acquaintance, he compiled a list of presumably interested people. He wrote to them about his find. This was not easy because with his limited schooling, he finds letter writing difficult and time-consuming. He got only one encouraging reply: from Dr. Landsverk, whose Landsverk Foundation deals precisely with Old Norse contacts with pre-Columbian America.

Fortunately, Professor Einar Haugen, Director of Scandinavian Studies at Harvard University, became involved in the Spirit Pond material. Dr. Haugen is a seasoned authority on the whole gamut of Nordic scholarship including runology. He undertook the preparation of a report on the Spirit Pond inscriptions for the State Museum in Augusta, Maine. His involvement is important because his analysis of the plaintext reflects expert knowledge of runic epigraphy and Nordic philology.[10]

My wife Joan and I were vacationing in northern New England and on coming home on 12 August 1971, I received a phone call from Card who told me about the find and expressed the hope that I was sufficiently interested to examine the Maine runestones. I invited him and Elliott to visit us on the evening of 13 August at our Brookline home. They brought two of the stones (SP-1 and SP-3) with them and explained that Landsverk had the remaining one on loan in California. (Later, after Landsverk returned SP-2, they let me examine it to my full satisfaction. Card placed prints of his photos of all three texts at my disposal, and I have been able to check all the problematic readings on the original stones.) Elliott wanted to know only one thing: What do the stones say? I tried to explain that inscriptions hundreds of years old—in exotic scripts and strange dialects—often have to be studied methodically and in painstaking detail before they yield their messages. This is not easy for a layman to understand. Carpentry has fewer pitfalls than runology. However, I was able to read for him VINLAND, HOOP (the name of the find-site), several numbers including "1010" and "1011" (neither of which, however, is the date when the inscriptions were written), and a few sundry words such as AHR "year" and names such as HAAKON.

Card and Elliott suggested we all go to Spirit Pond. We eagerly drove there the following morning, 14 August 1971. Without a guide it would have been almost impossible to find the place. The terrain is overgrown and full of obstacles, wet and dry. It is now state property. Elliott knew every inch of the wild tract as the constantly revisited haunts of his childhood. Card soon convinced me that the chart on SP-1 was a map of the Spirit Pond area with its nearby waterways and islands. Some of the latter, like the local Long Island, and the heartshaped Seguin Island, still retain the essential shapes accorded them on SP-1. We looked for traces of old structures, but found none. The heavy underbrush might, however, conceal features that we missed during our brief visit.

A few weeks later, the State of Maine ordered Elliott to return the stones which belonged to the state because he had found them on state property. This angered Elliott who had gone to trouble and expense in the matter, and by now realized the value of the stones. Being honest but proud, he reburied the stones near the find site, and informed the state that it could now let some other damned fool find them. To avoid extradition and prosecution, he fled secretly to Florida but maintained contact with Card.

The State of Maine had a good legal case, but Elliott had human rights. It was not a matter of absolute right versus absolute wrong, but a conflict of rights. A child or an ignorant fisherman might have chanced upon the stones and tossed them into the water to spend eternity in sand or slime. Elliott not only found the stones but recognized their importance and brought them to the attention of the authorities and indeed of the world. He had meanwhile turned down sums of money offered by dealers.

Early in January 1972, Card phoned me to tell me what was going on. I had been in Egypt during December 1971, and was unaware of the altercation between Elliott and his native state, and of his flight to Florida. Card informed me that a Philadelphia philanthropist was ready to pay $4500 to Elliott for delivering the stones to the State of Maine, if only some scholar would express the possibility of their being authentic. Card also told me that Elliott had placed a chart, indicating the exact spot where he had buried the stones, in the glove compartment of his car in case he should meet with a fatal accident while driving back to New England, so that the inscriptions could in any case be disinterred. I told Card to have the philanthropist phone me so that I could lend my support.

On Sunday evening, 9 January 1972, the long-distance operator rang to tell me there was a call from Philadelphia. The caller introduced himself as Mr. Lawrence M. C. Smith, and asked my opinion about the stones. I told him the final test of authenticity might require the passing of considerable time. (If in a quarter of a century none of the solecisms of the Spirit Pond runestones turn up elsewhere, they would probably be fakes, whereas, if the solecisms turn up on authentic runestones excavated during that time, they would prove to be genuine.) I added that in my judgment, there was a 50-50 chance that they were genuine. Mr. Smith replied that he considered $4500 a small amount for such good odds, and would put up the cash without delay.

The happy ending took place before the month was over. Elliott drove north, got the money, and turned over the stones to the state. On 9 February 1972, a Maine official delivered them to Professor Haugen for study with a view to preparing a professional report. Provision was also made to have Mr. William Young of the Boston Museum of Fine Arts perform the laboratory tests to determine the age of the carvings. The tests were completed in mid-June 1972.

Also on 9 February 1972, I gave an archaeological lecture at Brandeis University to report on my December trip to Egypt. Card had phoned a few days before to tell me the good news about the stones, and I took the opportunity to invite him and Elliott to my lecture, and to add a presentation of their own on Spirit Pond. Card showed slides of the stones, and of our visit to the find site on 14 August 1971. That was the first presentation of the material before an academic audience. There would be many others in the future. After the lecture, a Yankee lady asked Elliott (with a smile) whether he had written the runestones himself. His good-humored reply was: "If I can barely write English, how can I write runestones?"

Meanwhile Calvin Trillin brought the story to the attention of the sophisticates in an article called "U.S. Journal: Maine—Runes" in *The New Yorker* of 5 February 1972, pp. 70–74. So the cat was out of the bag, and the tortuous journey to the truth, a foregone conclusion.

Though Card and Elliott are thoroughly honest and reliable, their integrity does not rule out the possibility that the stones were planted at Spirit Pond sometime in this century by ethnocentric Scandinavians or plain pranksters. It was hoped that laboratory tests of the carved surface would tell whether the cutting is recent or old. The trouble is that when stones lie buried, their surface is not affected by the sun, air, and light that produce weathering on exposed stones. In June 1972, Mr. William Young informed me that while he was suspicious of the stones, he simply could not be sure on the basis of laboratory tests.

All this means that we shall have to analyze the internal evidence of the inscriptions against the background of outside sources. The reader himself has to judge what the internal and external evidence proves. I have weighed all viewpoints carefully. The evidence is complex but it gives us a definite answer. I do not want the reader to accept my conclusions on faith. The objective evidence, and not any dogmatic pronouncement, is what matters. I have tried (in Chapter VI) to clarify and simplify the primary evidence, so that the reader will be able to see and judge for himself.

THE MAPS

The following seven maps have been prepared by Dr. John C. Lawrenz.

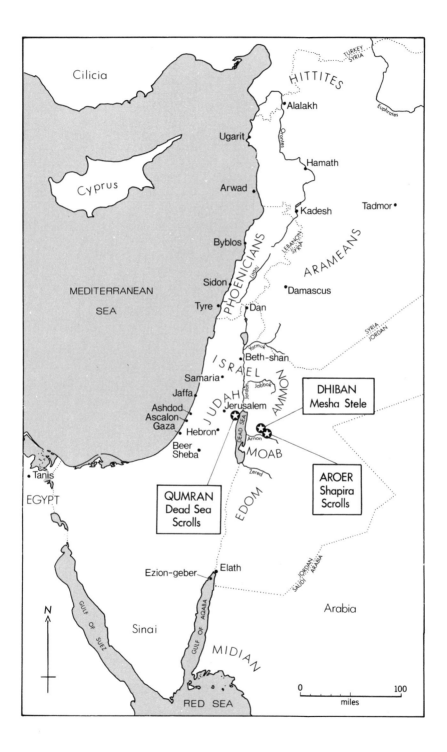

Cilicia

HITTITES

TURKEY
SYRIA

• Alalakh

Euphrates

Ugarit •

Hamath •

Cyprus

Arwad •

Tadmor •

• Kadesh

Byblos •

LEBANON-
SYRIA

MEDITERRANEAN
SEA

Sidon •

Litani

ARAMEANS

• Damascus

Tyre •

• Dan

PHOENICIANS

Orontes

SYRIA
JORDAN

Yarmuk

• Beth-shan

I S R A E L

Samaria •

AMMON

Jordan

Jaffa •

Jabbok

DHIBAN
Mesha Stele

J U D A H

Ashdod
Ascalon
Gaza

Jerusalem

DEAD SEA

Hebron •

Arnon

Beer
Sheba •

MOAB

QUMRAN
Dead Sea
Scrolls

Zered

AROER
Shapira
Scrolls

• Tanis

E D O M

EGYPT

Ezion-geber •

• Elath

JORDAN
SAUDI ARABIA

N

Arabia

GULF OF SUEZ

Sinai

GULF OF AQABA

MIDIAN

0   100
miles

RED SEA

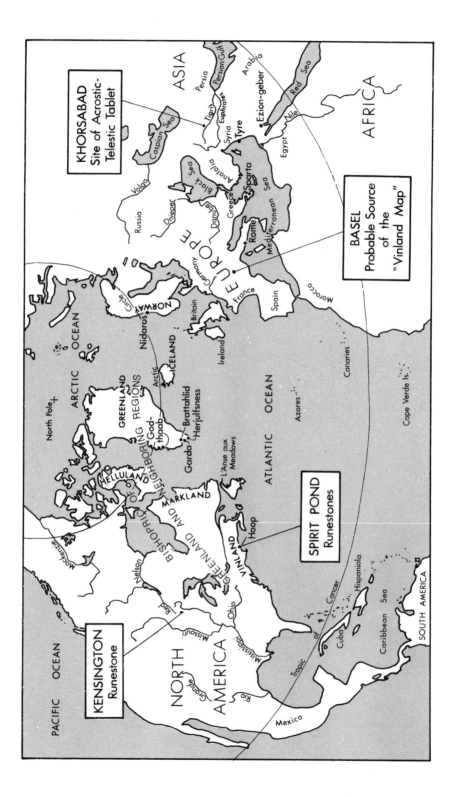

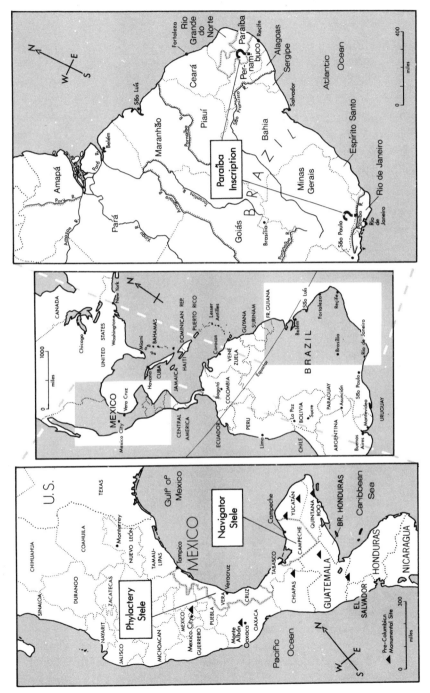

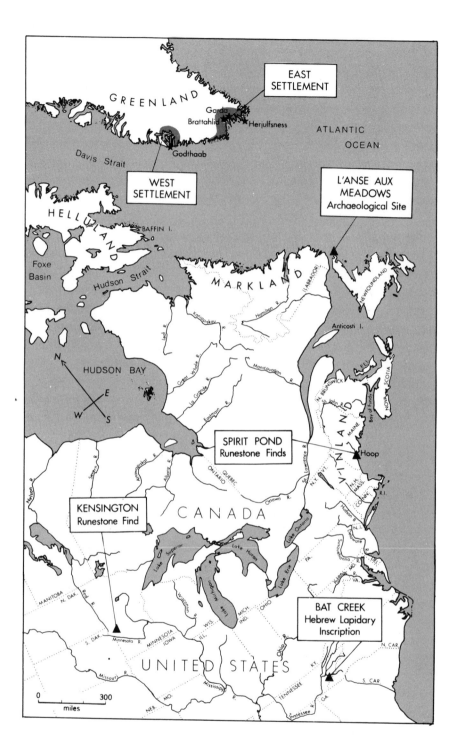

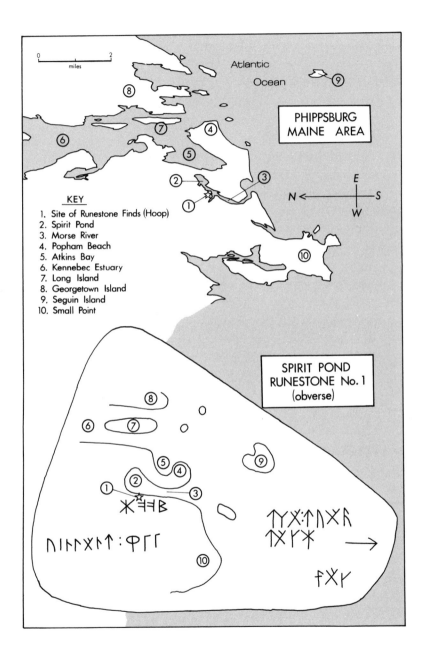

KEY

1. Site of Runestone Finds (Hoop)
2. Spirit Pond
3. Morse River
4. Popham Beach
5. Atkins Bay
6. Kennebec Estuary
7. Long Island
8. Georgetown Island
9. Seguin Island
10. Small Point

Atlantic Ocean

PHIPPSBURG
MAINE AREA

SPIRIT POND
RUNESTONE No. 1
(obverse)

CHAPTER II

Ancient Cryptograms

Neolithic man was as intelligent as we are. The repertoire of his materials shows that he traded across vast distances by land, and to some extent by sea. A Neolithic site in the Near East is likely to contain stones imported great distances from several directions. It may have lapis lazuli from Afghanistan and obsidian from the Aegean, including the island of Milos. Neolithic exports from islands imply marine trade. The Neolithic revolution that laid the foundations of subsequent civilization through animal husbandry, agriculture, and village society was no less significant than our recent achievements.

The beginnings of primitive writing may well lie in some remote Stone Age. But the real writing of texts with signs spelling out words in any identifiable language starts much later—around 3000 B.C.[11] It is not rare for men to be fifty years older than their youngest children. (I am fifty-three years older than my youngest child.) Only a hundred of such long (father-to-youngest-child) generations separate us from the dawn of actual writing in Mesopotamia 5,000 years ago.

Our contemporaries have split the atom, reached the moon, and brought color TV to the common man. The ancients, all through historic times (i.e., since 3000 B.C.), were not less talented than today's population, but they often expressed their intelligence in different ways. They manipulated language so deftly that it often takes modern scholars a long time to grasp the presence, let alone all the subtleties, of ancient riddles.

The key to Samson's riddle in Judges 14 eluded biblical experts throughout the ages until an ingenious Hebraist detected it in the twentieth century.[12]

Samson killed a lion and later found that bees had made a hive in its carcass, from which honey was dripping. He told nobody about the lion or the honey, but made a bet with some Philistines that within a week they could not solve the following riddle: "from the eater came forth food, and from the strong came forth sweet" (Judges 14:14). In translation there is no possible way to solve this riddle without being in on the secret about the lion and the bees. The Philistines found out the answer from his wife, who had nagged Samson into telling her. They won the bet by saying to Samson just before the time expired: "What is sweeter than honey and what is stronger than a lion (^{a}rī)?" (Judges 14:18). It happens that while ^{a}rī is well-known in the sense of "lion" it is at the same time a very rare word for "honey" preserved in Arabic, but nowhere else in extant Hebrew literature. The biblical text is cleverly constructed, because up to that point in the story, it refrains from calling the lion ^{a}rī. Instead it keeps the solution from the reader by calling the lion a k^{e}fīr ^{a}rāyôt (Judges 14:5) "a whelp of lionesses" and later an 'aryēh (14:8). "Honey" cannot be called k^{e}fīr ^{a}rāyôt nor 'aryēh; ^{a}rī "lion, honey" is artfully kept for the end.

Double entendre appears still earlier in the Gilgamesh Epic 11:48 where the Flood hero, Utnapishtim, does not want the public to know that the impending rainstorm will destroy them. So he announces that his god Ea is about to send a "rain of wheat," which they take to mean a rain beneficial for the crops. Unfortunately for them, kibâti in Babylonian means not only "wheat" but also "misfortune."[13]

Ancient writing was elitist from the start. Literacy tended to be limited to the professional scribes, so that script was a total mystery to the public at large. Since the scribes were the chosen few, rigorously trained in academies such as those in Mesopotamia and Egypt, they were not only clever, but enjoyed showing their cleverness in both plain and secret compositions. Moreover the script itself was considered a divine creation and the signs were regarded as having wondrous qualities. This also applied to the alphabet which has come down to us from the East Mediterranean where it began in the second millennium B.C. There is, for example, a mystical Jewish book called *Sēfer Yᵉṣîrāh* ("Book of Creation") according to which God first created the letters of the alphabet (along with numbers and words), and then through them went on to create the universe.[14] Mystery and magic were attributed to the alphabet from the start and kept reverberating even in Christian Europe as we shall note in our discussion of the Nordic runestones.

To understand how the ancients actually felt about the sophisticated uses of language, we must turn to the old texts themselves. The Proverbs of Solomon 1:6 states that the function of an education is "to understand a proverb and clever saying: the words of the wise and their riddles." For the sages it was not enough to handle plaintext. Plain language is for plain people. The elite must also master riddles and cryptograms, and grasp the deeper meaning subtly concealed beneath the surface meaning.

A common type of cryptography is encipherment by substitution. Examples of *atbash*, which is the commonest of the Hebrew substitution ciphers, occur in the Old Testament. *Atbash* consists of substituting the first letter (A) for the last letter (T) in the Hebrew alphabet, the second letter (B) for the next-to-the-last (Š, pronounced *sh*), and so forth:

cipher text: A B G D H W Z Ḥ Ṭ Y K L M N S ᶜ P Ṣ Q R Š T

plain text: T Š R Q Ṣ P ᶜ S N M L K Y Ṭ Ḥ Z W H D G B A

Two well-known examples of *atbash* appear in the original Hebrew text of Jeremiah, where ŠŠK[15] (25:26; 51:41) stands for BBL "Babylon" and LB QMY[16] (51:1) stands for KŚDYM "Chaldeans."[17] Another possible example has not hitherto been pointed out: Hiram I of Tyre was displeased with territory ceded to him by Solomon and so he called it ARṢ KBWL (1 Kings 9:13) which is usually translated "the Land of Kabul." While there is no way of explaining KBWL as Hebrew or Phoenician, the pejorative nature of the term is clear from the context, which bluntly states that Hiram did not like the land that Solomon gave him. It happens that KBWL by *atbash* stands for LŠPK "for the rubbish heap"[18] which would represent Hiram's feelings vividly: his ally Solomon had given him land fit for a dump.

Another type of cryptogram is effected by transposition. The letters are rearranged and have to be restored to their proper order by the cryptanalyst. A simple form of transposition is writing the letters in reverse order (e.g., NHOJ for "John"). Such a cryptogram appears as a test given to a student at Ugarit before 1200 B.C. in the Late Bronze Age. The cuneiform document is inscribed on a clay tablet and constitutes the earliest known school text for training scribes in cryptography. The student is instructed to unscramble four transposed letters. A line is then drawn across the tablet, below which the pupil solves the problem, signs his name and indicates that it is an examination. Here is the text:[19]

Transliteration	Translation
$r \bullet n \bullet l \bullet a$	*rnla* (are the letters transposed)
$m^c n$	Answer:
———————	———————
alnr	*alnr* (is the correct order)
ṣdqšlm	*Ṣdqšlm* (the student's name)
dlt	(examination) document

THE HEBREW ALPHABET AND ITS TRANSLITERATION

'	B	G	D	H	W	Z	Ḥ	Ṭ	Y	K
L	M	N	S	'	P	Ṣ	Q	R	Š	T

THE HEBREW "ATBASH" SUBSTITUTION CIPHER

cipher text:

plain text:

ΙΗΣΟΥΣ ΧΡΕΙΣΤΟΣ ΘΕΟΥ ΥΙΟΣ ΣΩΤΗΡ ΣΤΑΥΡΟΣ

The initial letters in a Christian Sibylline Oracle, which spell out the name and epithets of Jesus: "Jesus, Christ, God's Son, Saviour, Cross."

In antiquity as today, cryptographers and cryptanalysts had to be trained systematically. This Ugaritic tablet was for training a beginner. Mature cuneiform scribes could handle complex cryptograms, as we shall soon observe.

Alphabetic acrostics are quite common. There are many Old Testament examples, in which the first verse starts with A, the next with B, and so on, until the last which starts with the final letter of the Hebrew alphabet (T). There are variations on the theme; e.g., Psalm 119 consists of eight verses starting with A, followed by eight with B, and so on, until the final eight with T. Acrostics continue in post-biblical times in Hebrew, Greek, and Latin as well as in other languages. Sometimes the initial letters spell out the author's or scribe's name, or some phrase of importance to the writer. For instance, an early Christian Sibylline oracle in Greek reads smoothly as a religious composition, even though the author has seen to it that the initial letters of the lines spell out: IĒSOYS XREISTOS THEOY YIOS SŌTĒR STAYROS "Jesus Christ, God's Son, Saviour, Cross."[20] It is important to note that through Greek and Latin the ancient Mediterranean traditions of cryptography penetrated Christian Europe.

The key to a cryptogram may be indicated in the format. It is important to note indentations, blank spaces, and the like. There are acrostic compositions in Babylonian, in which the opening sign of the first line in each stanza is written at the far left. All other lines are indented. Accordingly one is naturally led to read the signs that stand out on the left, from top to bottom, and discover the acrostic.[21]

CUNEIFORM INDENTED ACROSTIC

This tablet illustrates the cryptographic function of the layout. The first sign of each section begins at the far left. By reading these initial signs down, we get the acrostic. Thus, the opening sign in line 1 is *a;* in line 3, *na;* in line 5, *ku.* They spell out *a-na-ku* "I (am)." (Reproduced from Craig 1895, plates 29–31)

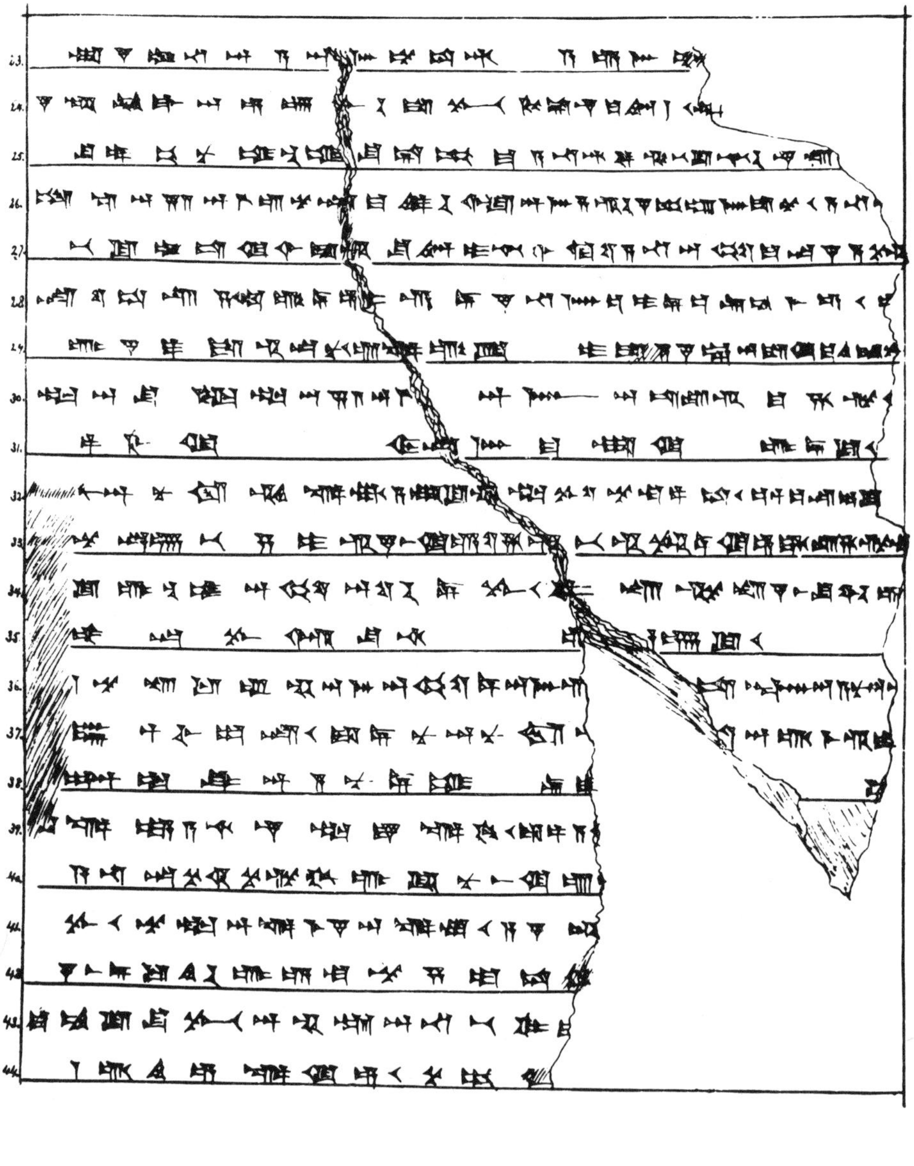

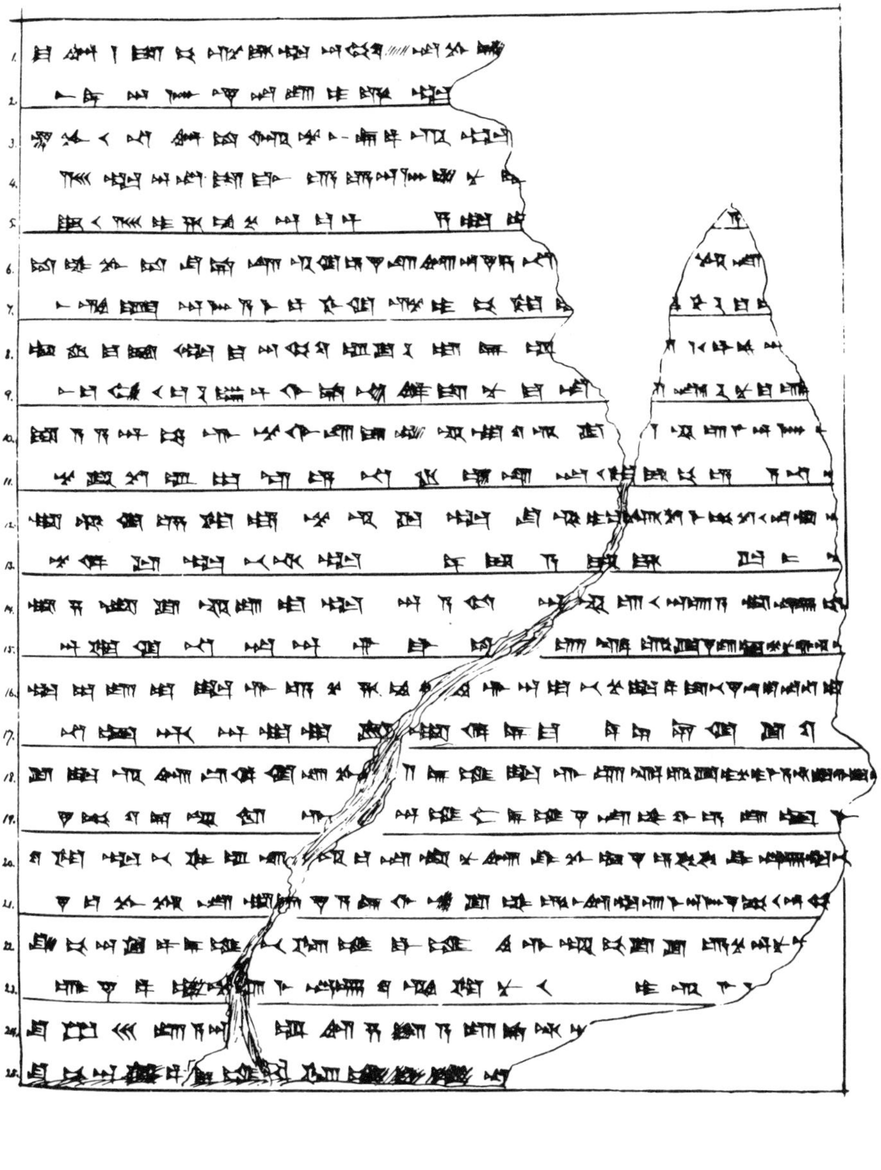

The "Babylonian Theodicy" (also known as the "Babylonian Koheleth") is a cuneiform composition of the mid second millennium B.C. It is divided into twenty-seven strophes of eleven lines each. All eleven lines in each strophe begin with the same syllabic sign. The twenty-seven initial syllables spell out the following sentence: *anâku Šaggil-kînam-ubbib mašmašu kâribu ša ili u šarrima* "I, Shaggil-kinam-ubbib, the conjuror, am a worshiper of God and King."[22] This type of acrostic message, spelling out the name and religious devotion of the scribe, continued to reverberate in Hebrew and Christian cryptography for millennia as we shall see in the chapters ahead.

The most interesting cryptograms in cuneiform literature are found in a tablet excavated by the University of Chicago in 1932 at Khorsabad, the Assyrian capital of King Sargon (722–705 B.C.). It cannot be later than the eighth-century B.C. It contains two poems, one on the obverse, the other on the reverse. The initial syllables of each poem constitute an acrostic that spells out the scribe's name and title.[23] The final syllables constitute, in each poem, a "telestic" spelling out his claim to pious devotion.[24] We shall presently be tracing the transmission and development of acrostic-telestic cryptograms in Jewish and medieval Christian circles. The tablet in transliteration reads as follows: obverse

1) šá-áš-ši abbê^{mes}-šú mut-lel-lu-ú e-tel-lu ^{d}asar-re

2) na-din u$_4$-mu ru-qu-ú-tu et-pe-šú te-le-'-e

3) bu-ul-lu-ṭu šu-ul-lu-mu i-tuk-ka ba-a-šu

4) ú-šar-ba-a ba-'-ú-la-a-tú šùm-ka as-mu

5) ⌈ú⌉-la-la u dun-na-mu-ú ⌈ú⌉-paq-qu ka-a-šá

6) [še-ma-t]a ik-ri-⌈bi⌉-šú-n[u] ta-[na]m-din li-i-pu

7) i[b-tar]-ra-a niší^{mes} mâti t[a-ni]t-ta-ka u$_4$-me-šam/ú

8) ši-kin na-piš-ti ú-ša[r-ra-ḫa] zi-kir-ka ṭa-a-bi/bé

9) a-na ^{md}nabû-ú-šeb-ši re-e-[ši m]u[t-ni]n-ni-i lib-ba-ši ṣu-lu-lu

1

Egyptian seagoing ship of about 2500 B.C.

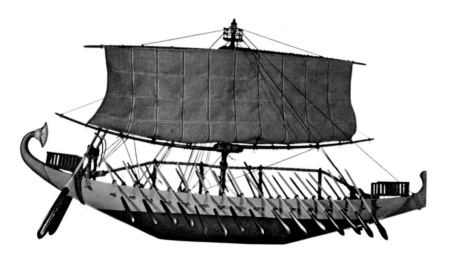

2

Egyptian seagoing ship from the time of Queen Hatshepsut, in the fifteenth century
B.C.

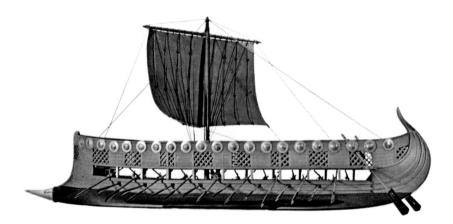

3

Phoenician warship of the bireme class, of about 700 B.C.

4

Phoenician seagoing ship of about 700 B.C.

5

Roman grain ship of about 200 A.D.

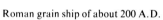

6

Sidonian merchantman of about the third century A.D.

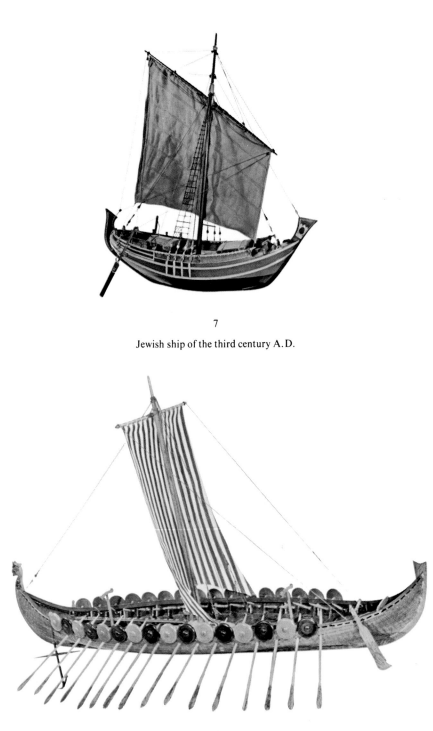

7

Jewish ship of the third century A.D.

8

Viking (Gokstad) ship of about the ninth century A.D.

10) ši-mat nišî^{me} li-ir-šá-a na-an-na-bu ki-si-it-ti

11) pi-ir-ú-šú a-na ma-ti-ma lil-bu-ru ma-ḫar-ka

---

12) 11 MU^{meš} e-liš za-ra-a là šakna re-eš mi-ḫi-il-ti

13) ù qí-it mi-ḫi-il-ti a-na šini-šú iš-šá-as-su-ú

reverse

1) šá-nu-du ti-iz-qa-ru[b]u-kúr ^dasar-re

2) na-a-bi kal mim-ma šum-[šú še-m]u-ú su-pe-e

3) bu-nu nam-ru-ti ma-l[i-k]u abbê^{meš}-š [u]

4) ú-šum-gal-lum la ma-ḫar [api]l ^dnu-dím-
[m]u[d]/[m]u[t]

5) ú-su-um ^dí-gì-gì be-el [né-me-q]í ḫ [a-mi-m]u gi-
mir uz-ni/né

6) šip-kát áš-ru u ki-gal-[lu qa-tuk-k]a kun-nu

7) ⌜ši-mat dum-qí ta-šá⌝-mu ^d[na-b] i-um e/si-nu-ú

8) [a-na ^{md}nabû-ú-š]eb-ši du-uš-m[i] -ka šu-ru-uk šá-
ṭa-pa

9) [ši-bu-ta liš-b] a-a lik-šu-du lit-tu-tú/liḫ

10) [pu-ḫu-ur(?) ku] -ul-la-tu lid-lu-lu qur-di-ka

---

11) [10 MU^{meš} e-liš za-r]a-a là šakna re-eš mi-ḫi-il-ti u
qí-it mi-ḫi-il-tú

12) [a-na šini-šú iš-šá-] as-su-ú

13) [   ] ⌜^{md}nabû⌝(?)-šùm-iddina mâr ^{lú}ka-nik
bâbi

Both the obverse and reverse are prayers on behalf of a man named Nabû-ušebši. The prayer on the obverse is addressed to Marduk (called "Asare" here), revered as the Creator. The prayer on the reverse is offered to Marduk's firstborn, Nabu, the god of the arts and sciences. The last line on the reverse is the colophon giving the scribe's (?) name. The tablet runs as follows in translation:

obv. 1) Sun of his fathers, exalted, the noble Asare
      2) Giver of long life, skilled, capable!
      3) It is yours to keep alive and healthy.
      4) Mankind magnifies your fitting name.
      5) The afflicted and the oppressed heed you
      6) You [hear] their prayer, you give offspring.
      7) The peoples of the land contemplate your praise every
         day.
      8) All living proclaim your good name.
      9) Let there be protection for Nabû-ušebši, the reverent
         suppliant
     10) That he may get what is destined for people: progeny
         and descendants
     11) That his seed may grow old before you forever.

     12) Eleven lines above ----- The beginning of the in-
         scription
     13) and the end of the inscription are to be read two ways.

rev. 1) Hero, lofty, firstborn of Asare
      2) Who has called everything into being, hearer of
         prayers
      3) Of shining countenance, counsellor of his fathers,
      4) Unrivaled ruler, heir of Nudimmud,
      5) Most fitting of the Igigi, lord of wisdom, who com-
         prehends all learning,
      6) The fashioning of the Place (= heaven?) and Under-
         world is established in your hand
      7) You decree a favored destiny, O --- Nabu.
      8) Give long life to ꜟNabuꜟ -ušebši, your slave,
      9) That he may have his fill of ripe old age and reach
         the golden years
     10) That al[l the world] (?) may praise your heroism.

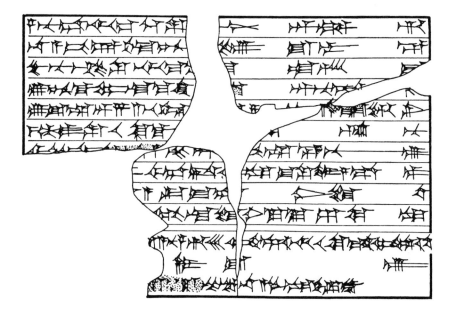

THE ACROSTIC-TELESTIC TABLET FROM KHORSABAD
This clay tablet of the eighth century B.C. is inscribed with the two earliest known acrostic-telestics. They constitute the prototype, in message content as well as cryptographic form, of the later acrostic-telestics until deep into the Middle Ages. (This facsimile, made by Professor W.G. Lambert, is reproduced from the *Journal* of the American Oriental Society, 88, 1968, p. 131, with the permission of Dr. Lambert and the editors of the *Journal*.)

11) [Ten lines above] - - - - - The beginning of the inscription

12) and the end of the inscription are to be [read two
ways].

13) [   ] Nabû (?)-šum-iddina, son of the Doorman.

The person for whom these two prayers were written is named
Nabû-ušebši in obv. 9 and rev. 8. His piety is expressed in obv. 9
in the words *re-e-ši mut-nin-ni-i* "the prayerful servant." His
name and professional title are written acrostically in each
prayer. If we read the opening syllable in the first eleven lines of
the obverse, from the top down, we get *ša na-bu-ú-ú-še-ib-ši a-ši-
pi* "belonging to Nabû-ušebši the exorcist." The same statement
is compressed acrostically into the first ten lines of the reverse: *ša
na-bu-ú-ú-šeb-ši [a-ši-pu]* "belonging to Nabû-ušebši [the exor-
cist]." (The same cuneiform sign stands for *šip* as required by the
horizontal text, or *šeb* as required by the vertical acrostic.) By
reading the final syllables of lines 1–11 on the obverse, from the
top down, we get the telestic: *re-e-šu mu-šá-pu-ú bé-lu-ti-ka* "the
servant who proclaims your lordship." The telestic at the end of
reverse 1–10 is: *re-e-šu mut-ni-nu-ú pa-liḫ-ka* "the prayerful servant who worships you."[25]

This acrostic-telestic of the eighth century B.C. anticipates
those in the Paraiba Stone and Vinland Map as to content. All
three texts contain a formula expressing the person's religious
devotion. In addition, the Khorsabad and Vinland texts share
another feature: the author's name appears in both the plaintext
and cryptogram.[26]

The Khorsabad tablet was not written to conceal the acrostic-
telestic from all but the chosen few. The scribe openly boasts of
his cleverness, telling the reader that the opening and closing
signs of the lines can be read two ways: vertically as well as horizontally. The reader is not alerted by any such statement in the
Paraiba Stone and Vinland Map, whose cryptograms (missed by

the "plaintext philologians" who first analyzed the texts) were detected only recently by trained cryptanalysts.

All of the old literary traditions made an honored place for cryptograms. Many, for example, have been left to us by ancient Egypt, whose scribes loved subtlety. However, the main traceable line of transmission to Western Europe starts with ancient Mesopotamia, reaches Canaan through the cuneiform scribes at centers like Ugarit, is spread by land and sea by Phoenicians and Hebrews, is embraced by Greeks and Romans as part of their Mediterranean heritage, and through them is passed on to Christian Europe via the church. The Canaanites (Phoenicians and Hebrews) carried the acrostic-telestic across the Atlantic Ocean in the sixth century B.C. The Roman Catholic priests of Scandinavia perpetuated the cryptographic tradition (including the acrostic-telestic) and carried it to America in the Middle Ages.

There are interesting clues in detail, to the chain of transmission. Thus the Vinland Map uses the name "Lysander" as the cryptographic key to the acrostic-telestic. Lysander was the Spartan general recalled by an enciphered message as related in Plutarch's *Lives* ("Lysander" 19).[27] The encipherment was effected by using a device called a *skytalē* in Greek. The sender and receiver of the secret message had identical staffs (or *skytalē*s). A long strip of writing material was wrapped spirally around the *skytalē* and then the text was written in straight lines (from one end of the *skytalē* to the other) so that the letters spanned the sections of the strip. Thus the writing appeared unintelligible when the strip was unwound from the *skytalē*. The receiver would have to rewind the strip on his identical *skytalē* to restore the plaintext. The Roman Catholic author of the Vinland Map belonged to the circle of educated Latinists with access to the story of Lysander's recall through a cryptographic message, from the Latin translation of Plutarch's *Lives*. Lysander's experience was appropriate, for the Vinland Map also tells how Bishop Henricus (the Latin name of the Nordic churchman Eirikr Gnupsson) was recalled from afar by his superiors.

The cryptograms we have mentioned so far are all embedded in plaintext. But sometimes the scribes felt no obligation to provide a meaningful cover text, and simply wrote their cryptograms in ways that make no plain sense. For instance, the runic text from Lindholm is inscribed on two surfaces of a bone object.[28] The message on one surface is intelligible: ek erilaR sa wīlagaR hā[i]teka "I Eril (= the runemaster) am called The Wily." But what is written on the other surface makes no plain sense: aaaaaaaaRRRnnn?bmuttt : alu : . Only the final word, *alu,* is translatable; it means "protection, amulet" and points to a magical interpretation of the letters that precede it. Such apparent gibberish is not always magical; it may constitute cryptograms for names, dates, and other items reserved for the elite.[29]

We are now ready to consider the inscriptions containing cryptograms that were written by pioneers who crossed the Atlantic before Columbus. The key texts turned up during the last hundred years and were studied by scholars unaware of long-forgotten cryptograms such as the acrostic-telestic. Unable to fathom the peculiarities of the documents, the consensus inclined understandably toward the easy way out: "all the texts are fakes." But as we have just seen, the acrostic-telestic tradition can be traced back to a scientifically excavated tablet of the eighth century B.C., whose authenticity and antiquity have not been, and will not be, questioned. To make of the Paraiba Stone a nineteenth-century forgery, is to attribute to an imposter, in 1872, knowledge that no professional scholar possessed until 1969 when Professor R. F. G. Sweet, of the University of Toronto, published his discovery of an acrostic-telestic in the Khorsabad tablet that had lain buried for over two and a half millennia until it was unearthed in 1932.[30]

The Khorsabad expedition was sent by the Oriental Institute of the University of Chicago. When the tablet was discovered in 1932, I happened to be a member of the University of Pennsylvania Museum expedition just a couple of miles away at Tepe Gawra. The Chicago and Pennsylvania teams visited back and forth and exchanged archaeological news frequently. But none of us realized that within forty years, the Khorsabad tablet would provide crucial background for establishing the links between the Old World and ancient America.

CHAPTER III

The Paraiba Inscription

The Paraiba text, like most ancient inscriptions, has difficulties that are being elucidated through continued study in the light of new related material. Some obscurities still remain. However, the general significance of the text has been clear from the start: it celebrates a voyage of Sidonian subjects who embarked at Ezion-geber in the nineteenth year of King Hiram and sailed around the Cape of Good Hope to Brazil, where the inscription turned up in 1872.[31]

The language belongs to the Canaanite group of very closely related dialects that include Phoenician and Hebrew. If we engage in finesse, we can subdivide Phoenician into many sub-dialects: Tyro-Sidonian (or South Phoenician), Byblian (Central Phoenician), Arwadian (North Phoenician), Cypriote, Punic (West Phoenician), etc. By the same token there are many varieties of Hebrew, even in the Bible itself—let alone in the diverse inscriptions from Judah in the south and from Israel in the north of Palestine. All forms of Hebrew and Phoenician were mutually intelligible, and dialect mixture in the border areas was normal.

The dialect mixture in the Paraiba text has been explained in different ways. It has been suggested that while the Ezion-geber fleet was under Sidonian sponsorship, the personnel were seamen recruited from various Northwest Semitic areas: Phoenician, Hebrew, Aramean, and perhaps also Moabite (Transjordanian), and Edomite (for Ezion-geber is in Edom).[32]

Professor A. Van den Branden has offered another explanation that has much in its favor.[33] The strong Hebrew component, tinged with Phoenicianisms, suggests to him that the dialect of the scribe (and probably the crew) stemmed from the southern border of the Sidonian realm, where the population had close affinities with the Hebrews. This is confirmed by the message in the telestic which indicates that the scribe (and perhaps also some of the crew) worshiped the God of Israel.

The script of the Paraiba inscription fits a date of about 500 B.C. better than earlier or later periods. But there is an important factor which must be taken into consideration. All of our copies stem from Ladislau Netto's transcripts of the master copy, which itself was only a copy of the original. Netto made his facsimiles with pen and ink on paper. Ink or pencil transcriptions tend to round off points and introduce curves, and thus alter the lapidary style of an ancient scribe incising letters with a chisel on stone. Published copies of the same Canaanite text may look hundreds of years apart because of the different copyists' styles. Van den Branden notes that the same medallion from Carthage looks like an eighth century B.C. text in Donald Harden's copy,[34] but like a sixth century B.C. text as copied in Donner-Röllig.[35] There is little doubt that Netto, as a result of his intensive study of Phoenician and Hebrew, was influenced by the letter forms in the published facsimiles of the texts and in the charts available to him. So while I prefer to date the Paraiba text in the reign of Hiram III (553–533 B.C.) partly on the basis of the script, Van den Branden's preference for the reign of Hiram I (tenth century B.C.) cannot be ruled out by hyperfinesse in analyzing the letter forms as though they were before us on the original stone.[36]

The 534–531 B.C. date (i.e., from Hiram III's nineteenth year to two and a fraction years later, as specified in the text) fits the

MODERN HEBREW LETTER	PARAIBA (ca. 530 B.C.)	BAT CREEK (ca. A.D. 100)
א		
ב		
ג		
ד		
ה		
ו		
ז		
ח		
ט		
י		
כ		
ל		
מ		
נ		
ס		
ע		
פ		
צ		
ק		
ר		
ש		
ת		

historic picture well. The route around the Cape of Good Hope had been activated around 600 B.C. by Phoenician sailors sponsored by Pharaoh Necho II (Herodotus, *Histories* 4:42)[37] so that in the sixth century B.C. the circumnavigation of Africa was known. That it was not only known but actually used for reaching the Atlantic from the Near East in 534–531 B.C. is supported by the fact that the Sidonians under Hiram III were allies of Cyrus the Great, who controlled the Levant including Phoenicia. However, the Carthaginians who dominated the western half of the Mediterranean were able to block the Strait of Gibraltar to their rivals and enemies including the Phoenicians who were vassals of Cyrus.

The purpose of the voyage can be accounted for in different ways. The situation in Canaan during the last third of the sixth century B.C. was not altogether comfortable for the natives. The Phoenicians were subject to the powerful Achaemenian Empire of the Medes and Persians, while the impoverished Judeans were struggling to establish their Second Commonwealth within the framework of that Empire. The crew may have been looking for an easier life elsewhere, but it is more likely that the fleet of ten ships had been dispatched to support, and perhaps also to set up, operational bases on both sides of the Atlantic for trade and especially for access to raw materials. The one ship that reached South America may have been accidentally carried across the Atlantic by winds and currents (as actually happened to Pedro Cabral in A.D. 1500). On the other hand, it is possible that the entire voyage was planned, including the Atlantic crossing. While a certain number of transoceanic voyages were accidental (and some important discoveries were made that way), most ancient voyages were intentional, along known routes, to known destinations and for specific purposes.[38] The most likely reason for sailing to Brazil was the quest for minerals, particularly iron, which Brazil has in profusion and which was vital in the Iron Age (after 1200 B.C.) for nations atune to the technology and progress of the times.

It is simplest to follow most of the discussion of the Paraiba text, in Latin transliteration. The Canaanite alphabet consists of twenty-two letters (all originally consonants) which can be rendered unequivocally by Latin letters with the help of a few diacritical marks for some peculiar Semitic sounds. Those who know Hebrew will want to read also the transcription into modern Hebrew letters. At several junctures it will be necessary for the reader (whether or not he knows any ancient scripts or languages) to refer to the facsimile of the text in the original old Canaanite letter forms. The physical layout of the text is, for example, cryptographically significant. Furthermore, as the facsimile shows, all the letters are run together with no space between words. Accordingly some differences of opinion are to be expected concerning the division of the text into words. (They-wenttogether," depending on context, could stand for "they went to get her" as well as "they went together.") In a few cases some uncertainty remains regarding word division. Another source of doubt stems from similarity between some of the letter forms. D and R resemble each other somewhat, and so do W and K; but the only really troublesome pair are L and N, which are often hard to distinguish.

1) NḤN' BN KN^CN MṢDN MHQRT HMLK SḤR HŠLK-

2) N' 'L 'Y Z RḤQT 'RṢ HRM WNŠT BḤR L^CLYWNM

3) W^CLYWNT BŠNT TŠ^CT W^CŚRT LḤRM MLKN' 'BR

4) WNHLK M^CṢWN GBR BYM SP WNNS^C ^CM 'NYT ^CŚRT

5) WNHYH BYM YḤDW ŠTM ŠNM SBB L'RṢ LHM WNBDL

6) MYD B^CL WL' NH 'T ḤBRN' WNB' HLM ŠNM ^CŚR

7) MTM WŠLŠT NŠM B'Y ḤDT 'Š 'N KY MT ^CŚRT 'BR

8) ḤBLTY' ^CLYWNM W^CLYWNT YḤNN'

The English translation is:

1) We are sons of Canaan from Sidon, from the city where a merchant (prince) has been made king. He dispatched
2) us to this distant island, a land of mountains. We sacrificed a youth to the celestial gods
3) and goddesses in the nineteenth year of Hiram, our King. *Abra!*
4) We sailed from Ezion-geber into the Red Sea and voyaged with ten ships.
5) We were at sea together for two years around Africa. Then we got separated
6) by the hand of Baal and we were no longer with our companions. So we have come here, twelve
7) men and three women, into one island, unpopulated because ten died. *Abra!*
8) —May the celestial gods and goddesses favor us!

For reasons that will be spelled out, we can only be certain that lines 1–3 and 8 are meant to be taken literally in detail. Lines 1–3 tell us that the crew consists of Canaanites from Sidon, sent to a far-off mountainous land by their mercantile King Hiram in his nineteenth year. On that occasion they made a human sacrifice to the gods for the success of the expedition.

The text follows a format now known from other ancient Northwest Semitic inscriptions. Line 1 opens with (1) identifying the people concerned; then comes (2) the statement of what is being commemorated; and finally (3) the gods are exhorted to bestow their favor. The Mesha Stone, known since 1868, may have followed this format, but since the end is lost, only the first and second sections could have been imitated in 1872. The Azitawadd text preserves all three sections, but since it was not discovered until 1946, it could not have served as a model in 1872.

The mention of a sacrifice and date is duplicated in many Northwest Semitic texts.[39]

The scribe had to use his ingenuity in wording the text because

1) נחנאבנכנענמצדנמהקרתהמלכסחרהשלכ

2) נאאלאיזרחקתארצהרמונשתבחרלעליונמ

3) ועליונתבשנתתשעתועשרתלחרממלכנאאבר

4) ונהלכמעצונגברביםספוננסעעמאניתעשרת

5) ונהיהבימיחדושתמשנמסבבלארצלחמונבדל

6) מידבעלולאנהאתחברנאונבאהלמשנמעסר

7) מתמושלשתנשמבאיחדתאשאנכימתעשרתאבר

8) חבלתיאעליונמועליונתיחננא

The Paraiba Inscription transliterated into modern Hebrew letters. As in the original, the text is not divided into words, and no "final forms" of the letters are used.

1) נחנא בן כנען מצדן מהקרת המלך סחר השלכ-

2) נא אל אי ז רחקת ארץ הרם ונשת בחר לעליונם

3) ועליונת בשנת תשעת ועשרת לחרם מלכנא אבר

4) ונהלך מעצון גבר בים סף וננסע עם אנית עשרת

5) ונהיה בים יחדו שתם שנם סבב לארץ לחם ונבדל

6) מיד בעל ולא נה את חברנא ונבא הלם שנם עסר

7) מתם ושלשת נשם באי חדת אש אן כי מת עשרת אבר

8) חבלתיא עליונם ועליונת יחננא

The Paraiba Inscription transcribed into modern Hebrew letters, divided into words, and with "final forms" used at the end of words in the case of the letters which have special final forms.

of cryptograms that imposed obstacles he had to surmount. This impelled him to draw on whatever options of spelling and vocabulary were available in his day. None of his usages must be dated after the sixth century B.C. and some of the peculiarities that cast doubt on the text a century ago are features now attested in other inscriptions of the sixth century B.C. and in some cases are also traceable back to the Bronze Age.

The language is entirely Northwest Semitic. Many grammatical features, in addition to practically all of the vocabulary, are common in Hebrew: e.g., the causative conjugation with preformative *h-* (HMLK "he was made king" and HŠLK "dispatched" in line 1). Some of the features occur sporadically in Hebrew, but are normal in other Canaanite dialects; thus the suffix of feminine singular nouns and adjectives in the absolute state is -*t*; thus RHQT "distant" (feminine singular) in line 2 as in Phoenician, Moabite, etc. The regular narrative tense is the imperfect preceded by *w-*: WNŠT "we set, offered, sacrificed" (line 2), WNHLK "we went, sailed" (line 4), WNNS^C "we journeyed, voyaged" (line 4), WNBDL "we were separated" (line 5), WNB' "we have come" (line 6). The jussive is used not only for imprecations (thus YHNN' "may they favor us," line 8), but with WL' expresses negative narration (as in Job 23:11): WL' NH "we were not" (line 6), as opposed to WNHYH "we were" in line 5.

The first person plural pronoun ends in -*ā* as in Aramaic. The independent form is NHN' "we" (line 1). The suffixed form is written -N'; possessive: MLKN' "our king" (line 3), accusative: HŠLKN' "he dispatched us" (lines 1–2) and YHNN' "may they favor us" (line 8).

The numerals are especially interesting. As in Hebrew, Ugaritic, etc., the "correct" gender always characterizes "1" and "2." Thus HDT "1" (line 7) modifies a feminine noun and ends in feminine -*t,* and ŠNM "2" in masculine ŠNM ^{C}ŠR "12" (line 6) contrasts with ŠTM "2" (line 5) which is feminine. However, the numbers from "3" to "10" inclusive may have suffixed -*t* with nouns of either gender. This runs against normal Hebrew usage where the numerals from "3" to "10" inclusive, ending in -*t*, as a rule accompany masculine but not feminine nouns. Yet there are some Old Testament examples of these numerals in -*t* with feminine nouns as in the Paraiba text (e.g., 'NYT ^{C}ŠRT "10 ships" in line 4). Thus ŠLŠT "3" referring to "women" is found not only in line 7 but also in Genesis 7:13 (similarly Job 1:4).

The most emphatic objection raised by the nineteenth century critics was to the numeral "19" written TŠ^{C}T W^{C}ŠRT in line 3. The presence of -*t* in both the unit (TŠ^C-T "9") and the ten (^{C}ŠR-T "10") was then unheard of in Northwest Semitic. Meanwhile this construction has turned up abundantly in Ugaritic, but only in publications since 1957.[40] Van den Branden 1968 (p. 6) calls attention to a still closer parallel geographically; in a north Hebrew ostracon from Samaria published in 1964, BŠT HTŠ^{C}T H^{C}ŠRT "in the 19th year" occurs with both numerals ending in -*t* in a year date as in the Paraiba inscription.

The one word left untranslated, ḤBLTY' (line 8), is difficult but a tentative interpretation can be ventured. Dr. Lienhard Delekat takes ^{C}LYWNM as the name of a male deity, and ^{C}LYWNT as his female counterpart.[41] This is possible, especially in the light of Hebrew 'LHYM, the commonest word for "God" which is singular in meaning in spite of the plural suffix which ends in -*m*. If these two celestial deities are the patron gods of the seamen, ḤBLTY' might be a dual signifying "The 2 (divine) Mariners," recalling the second element in expressions like masculine ḤMWR ḤMRTYM "1 ass, 2 asses"[42] or feminine RḤM RḤMTYM "1 girl, 2 girls."[43]

The seemingly strange series of numbered items in lines 4–7 is a cryptogram confirming the date (year "19") by listing items which total twice 19 = 38. This method of confirming dates might have been (but in fact was not) surmised from the age-old Near Eastern love of doubling, especially numbers, but even other items, through the dual. (The idiomatic reply to the Arabic greeting *marḥaba* "welcome" is *marḥabatèn* "twice welcome.") The nature of our cryptogram was actually clarified through extraneous sources, remote—as so often happens in the case of breakthroughs—in time and place. The cryptographic confirmation of dates, by doubling the date numbers, reverberates in runic inscriptions (Chapters V and VI).[44]

The date cryptogram is set off between the 'BR at the end of line 3 and the 'BR at the end of line 7. Thus 'BR—'BR is a cryptographic indicator. 'BR can be pronounced *abra,* and "abra—abra" calls to mind the magic word "abra-cad-abra." As we shall note in another cryptogram in this text (namely, the acrostic-telestic), letter counts are significant, and the fact that there are exactly 24 letters in the final line may supply the missing -*cad*- of "abra-cad-abra." The conventional Hebrew number system is as follows:

ט	ח	ז	ו	ה	ד	ג	ב	א
9	8	7	6	5	4	3	2	1

צ	פ	ע	ס	נ	מ	ל	כ	י
90	80	70	60	50	40	30	20	10

ת	ש	ר	ק
400	300	200	100

The normal numerical values of the Hebrew letters.

A	B	G	D	H	W	Z	Ḥ	Ṭ
1	2	3	4	5	6	7	8	9

Y	K	L	M	N	S	ᶜ	P	Ṣ
10	20	30	40	50	60	70	80	90

Q	R	Š	T
100	200	300	400

In this system, "24" is written "KD" (i.e., K = 20 + D = 4) and is pronounced *cad,* which may represent the -cad- in "abracadabra."

If we add the numbers in lines 4–7

10	ships	(line 4)
2	years	(line 5)
12	men	(line 6)
3	women	(line 7)
1	island	(line 7)
10	who died	(line 7)

we get as the total   38
which is twice the year date "19." (Compare the "24" numbered items in the Kensington Stone confirming the numerals in the date, which total "12.")

Two expressions in this cryptogram are of importance in authenticating the Paraiba inscription. No one correctly read, let alone translated, the now crystal clear idiom YD BᶜL "hand of Baal = divinely decreed fate, destiny," until 1968. In 1939 YD BᶜL in this sense appeared for the first time in a published Phoenician text from Cyprus.[45] The words immediately following YD BᶜL are WL' NH "and we were not" with a special formation (W + negative L' + jussive verb) to express negated past time, never before recognized in Hebrew or other Northwest Semitic dialects. Because of the Paraiba text, it was recognized for the first time in Job 23:11.[46] It is irrational to ascribe to an unidentified (and purely hypothetical) 1872 forger an idiom unknown until 1939 and a rare negated tense unanalyzed in the Bible until 1968.

Since the scribe's aim, between the two *abra*s, was to compose a numerical cryptogram with items totaling "38," we should not expect historical accuracy. We cannot be sure that there were exactly 10 ships that rounded Africa in 2 years, carrying 12 men and 3 women to 1 island where 10 had died. At least some of the numerals are contrived. Certainly the "1" of "1 island" is artificial because "1" is not common in ancient Northwest Semitic dialects, in expressions where we use in English the indefinite article.[47] Moreover the "10" who died (line 7) should not be construed literally. It was Lienhard Delekat who first translated MT ^cŚRT correctly as "ten died."[48] Subsequently it emerged that this entry was evoked to mark the close of the cryptogram. In the Kensington Stone "24" is obtained by adding numerals down to and including the final entry of "10 men red with blood and dead." All this suggests that the "10" dead in both texts is cryptographic and not meant to be taken as historic fact.

The presence of another cryptogram is indicated by the layout of the Paraiba text. A glance at the facsimile shows that the scribe ends lines before the space runs out. This is true starting with the very first line on which there is not only room enough for completing the last word (HŠLKN'), which he spreads over two lines against all the academic rules, but room also for the next three words ('L 'Y Z) as well. The layout therefore alerts the reader to look for a cryptogram. An examination of the letters opening the eight lines confronts us with a pattern: NNWWW-MMH, hinting that the lines end where they do, to produce this series of initial letters. Can each initial letter be the cryptographic indicator for its line? If so, the ordinary numerical values cannot be intended, because since in the common system (cited above) N = 50, a fiftieth letter is out of the question in lines 1 and

כ	י	ט	ח	ז	ו	ה	ד	ג	ב	א
11	10	9	8	7	6	5	4	3	2	1

ת	ש	ר	ק	צ	פ	ע	ס	נ	מ	ל
22	21	20	19	18	17	16	15	14	13	12

The numerical values of the Hebrew letters as used to indicate the key in each line of the Paraiba Inscription.

1) ‏נחנא בן כנען מצדן מהקרת המלך סחר השלכ-‏   ‏(נ = 14‏

2) ‏נא אל אי ז רחקת ארץ הרם ‏ונשת בחר לעליונם‏   ‏(נ = 14‏

3) ‏ועליונת בשנת תשעת ועשרת לחרם מלכנא אבר‏   ‏(ו = 6‏

4) ‏ונהלך מעצון גבר בים סף וננסע עם אנית עשרת‏   ‏(ו = 6‏

5) ‏ונהיה בים יחדו שתם שנם סכב לארץ לחם ונבדל‏   ‏(ו = 6‏

6) ‏מיד בעל ולא נה את חברנא ונבא הלם שנם עסר‏   ‏(מ = 13‏

7) ‏מתם ושלשת נשם באי חדת אש אן כי מת עשרת אבר‏   ‏(מ = 13‏

8) ‏חבלתיא עליונם ועלינת יחננא‏   ‏(ח = 8‏

נ	צ	נ	מ	ב	ת	א	ל
8	7	6	5	4	3	2	1
ק	ו	כ	י	מ	ו	א	ו

נ	צ	ל	נ	א	כ	ב	מ	ת
6	4	5	7	3	8	2	י
ק	ו	י	ס	א	כ	י	ו

SOLUTION OF THE PARAIBA ACROSTIC-TELESTIC

The key (on the left) indicates the letter-count from both ends. The acrostic and telestic letters are underlined. At the lower right are the acrostic and telestic in 1-2-3-4-5-6-7-8 order; at the lower left they are unscrambled in 1-2-8-3-7-5-4-6 order, which converts them from anagrams into plaintext.

2, which have only 30 and 31 letters respectively. The same holds for lines 6 and 7, which have 31 and 32 letters respectively, ruling out the value of M = 40 in the common system.

Another numerical system comes to mind: the one whereby each letter stands for one unit higher than the preceding letter, from the 1st letter (A = 1) to the final or 22nd letter (T = 22):

A	B	G	D	H	W	Z	Ḥ	Ṭ	Y	K
1	2	3	4	5	6	7	8	9	10	11

L	M	N	S	ʿ	P	Ṣ	Q	R	Š	T
12	13	14	15	16	17	18	19	20	21	22

This is the common system in Greek, where the first letter alpha = 1, and so forth, until the final or 24th letter omega = 24. In Hebrew it has been known so far only in alphabetic acrostics, starting with the Bible.[49] The simplest examples are compositions of 22 verses, the first starting with A (= 1), the second with B (= 2) and so forth until the final 22nd verse which starts with T (= 22). We shall apply this system to the Paraiba text, from both ends, to see whether there is a cryptogram on either side, or on both sides simultaneously. The one obtained by reckoning from the beginning of the lines we shall call the acrostic, and the one obtained by reckoning from the end of the lines we shall call the telestic. On the far right, we shall give the numerical position of the initial letter in the alphabet as the cryptographic key, and underline the letters obtained by counting that number in from both ends.

Line	Key
1) NHN' BN KN^{c}N MṢDN̲ MHQRT HMLK SḤR HŠLK -	(N = 14
2) N''L 'Y Z RHQT 'RṢ HRM W̲NŠT BHR L^{c}LYWNM	(N = 14
3) W^{c}LYWN̲T ḂŠNT T̃Š^{c}T W^{c}S̃RT LḤṚM MLK̲N''BR	(W = 6
4) WNHLK M̲^{c}SWN GBR BYM SP WNNS$^{c\ c}$M' NẎT ^{c}S̃RT	(W = 6
5) WNHYH B̲YM YḤDW ŠTM ŠNM SBB L'RṢ LḤM̲ WNBDL	(W = 6
6) MYD B^{c}L WL' NH 'T̲ HBRN' W̲NB' HLM ŠNM ^{c}S̃R	(M = 13
7) MTM WŠLŠT NŠM B'Y ḤDT 'Š ̲'N KY MT ^{c}S̃RT 'BR	(M = 13
8) ḤBLTY' ^{c}L̲YWNM W^{c}LYW̲NT YḤNN'	(Ḥ = 8

The acrostic letters are:

N	Ṣ	N	M	B	T	'	L
1	2	3	4	5	6	7	8

and the telestic letters are:

Q	W	K	Y	M	W	'	W
1	2	3	4	5	6	7	8

Neither the acrostic nor telestic letters make any sense in 1-2-3-4-5-6-7-8 order. But both make quite appropriate sense simultaneously, only in 1-2-8-3-7-5-4-6 order, which yields:

acrostic:	N	Ṣ	L	N	'	B	M	T
	1	2	8	3	7	5	4	6
telestic:	Q	W	W	K	'	M	Y	W

Both make sense, as soon as we divide them into words. The acrostic NṢLN' B-MT means "We have been saved from Death," while the telestic QWW K 'M YW means "Trust only Yaw (= Yahweh, God)."

The phraseology and construction of the telestic message are paralleled in biblical usage. The root of the plural imperative QWW "trust, wait for, hope in, have faith in" is *qāwā*, which can take God's name as an accusative object (without any preposition or particle): QWYTY YHWH (Psalm 40:2; 130:5) "I trusted Yahweh." K 'M (pronounced *kī 'im*) "only" usually follows a negative in Hebrew; but in Job 42:8 (note also Genesis 40:14), it is used without the negative as in the Paraiba text. The variant spellings, with the vowel letter –Y (= KY in line 7), or without the vowel letter –Y (= K in the telestic), were both at the scribe's disposal depending on whether he needed the longer or shorter form in the cryptograms. In line 7, KY had to be spelled with two letters so that the cryptographic key (M = 13) would direct the reader to the right telestic letter (i.e., ' - aleph - which is the 13th letter from the end of the line). Here, in the telestic message, the whole declaration of faith had to be compressed into eight letters (which rules out KY, for it would raise the number of letters to nine). Spelling *kī* with the one letter K is normal Phoenician orthography; spelling it KY is normal Hebrew orthography. The scribe needed flexibility for composing his cryptograms which he concealed beneath a plaintext. The interesting thing is that he never misspells (as cryptographers in other traditions often do), but instead draws on the varying usages available to him in the sixth century B.C.[50] The message of the acrostic-telestic is a declaration of faith and piety, continuing a tradition attested in the eighth century acrostic-telestic from Khorsabad.

YW is the oldest form of the divine name that usually appears as YHWH "Yahweh." It is embedded in the name of the mother of Moses: YW-KBD "Jochabed"[51] but it first appears in the written records of Canaan in a mythological text of the Late Bronze Age, which states that YW . 'L (corresponding exactly to the Hebrew name YW-'L "Joel") is the son of the head of the pantheon.[52]

The acrostic message is written in complete accordance with attested usages. NSL means "was/were rescued" in Hebrew, while the first person plural suffix -N' "we" is consistently used in the plaintext. B- "from" is frequent in Ugaritic, and since the decipherment of Ugaritic has been detected in all of the Northwest Semitic languages including Hebrew. MT "Mot," the god of Death in Ugaritic mythology, is now fully recognized in the Bible. Nineteenth-century scholarship did not reckon with Mot as a deity. To consider this the work of an 1872 forger implies that he knew of twentieth-century developments in the study of Canaanite religion and expressed them in a complex acrostic-telestic, first rediscovered after centuries of oblivion in the 1970s.

The acrostic and the telestic provide parallelism, which typifies Northwest Semitic style: Mot, the god of death, is contrasted with Yaw/Yahweh the God of life. This dualism was particularly in the air during the Persian period, when Zoroastrianism stressed the antithesis between the evil god (Ahriman) and the good god (Ahuramazda). There is also parallelistic balance between thankfulness for *past* salvation, and the declaration of *future* trust in God.

The religion that appears in the plaintext is Canaanite paganism. Fate comes "from the hand of Baal" (line 6), the most active god in the Canaanite pantheon. The references in lines 2-3 and 8 to "the celestial gods and goddesses" is polytheistic paganism. But in the telestic, the scribe reveals himself as a Yahwist.

The biblical background for a Yahwistic Hebrew aboard a seagoing ship with pagan passengers and crew, is provided by the Book of Jonah, which reflects conditions around the seventh century B.C.—about a hundred years before the Paraiba inscription. Jonah is represented as the only Jew aboard a vessel bound for Tarshish: the westernmost land in the then-known world. A storm, taken to be the manifestation of divine wrath, threatens the ship and all aboard with destruction. The prayers of the crew prove to be of no avail, and the last hope for the vessel depends on Jonah, who instead of praying, is sleeping belowdecks. After the captain wakes him, it is determined by lot that he is the guilty party. He then confesses that the storm is raging on account of him, for he had offended God. He identifies himself thus: "I am a Hebrew and I fear Yahweh, God of the Heavens, who made the sea and dry land" (Jonah 1:9). He assures his fellow voyagers that if they throw him overboard, the storm will end (verse 12). The pagans, who are a humane group of people, reluctantly follow his instructions and the storm abates (verse 15). It is interesting to note that this is human sacrifice for the welfare of a ship at sea, which is what we find in the Paraiba inscription;[53] the Sidonian crew "sacrificed a youth to the celestial gods and goddesses" for the welfare of their marine mission.

The reader will find Ezekiel 27 a vivid description of Phoenician navigation in the sixth century B.C. (only about fifty years before the Paraiba text) on the high seas, on bold and profitable missions, through employing international personnel.

The phenomenon of "dissimulation" (concealing one's identity when revealing it might be harmful) may crop up in any land and in any period. But in Iran it has been a way of life, institutionalized to this day under the name of *taqiyya* or *ketmân*. It is described perfectly in the biblical Book of Esther, which is a novelette set in Susa, Iran, during the reign of Xerxes I (485–465 B.C.). The hero, Mordecai, is a Jew in the King's service, who kept his Jewish identity secret until it leaked out in a moment of carelessness (Esther 3:4). He instructs Esther not to tell even her husband, King Xerxes, that she is Jewish (2:10). But when a crisis arises that threatens the Jewish people, they do everything in their power to save them (4:13–16). The story brings out clearly that in such a system, though minorities may dissimulate, what is most precious to them is their ethnoreligious identity.

It is interesting to note that when the non-Jewish majority is threatened by Jewish action, the non-Jews "pretend to be Jews"[54] because of "fear" (8:16). This is still the case in Iran, where members of religious minorities (especially the Bahais) pose as Shiite Muslims. Yet the latter, who are the official majority, may pose as Sunnite Muslims when making the pilgrimage to Mecca where the Sunnite Arabs can be dangerously hostile to Shiites.

During the Achaemenian period (6th–4th centuries B.C.) dissimulation was very much in the atmosphere. Our scribe fits into this picture. Overtly he is Baalist pagan like his Sidonian masters and colleagues. But in his heart he is a Yahwist and expresses his credo "Trust only Yaw/Yahweh." His public image is in the plaintext, while his true self is hidden in the cryptogram.

The known record of Phoenician and Hebrew sailors working together in naval exploits, starts with Hiram I and Solomon in the tenth century B.C.[55] But Herodotus in the fifth century B.C. tells us that the main contingent of the Achaemenian Mediterranean fleet was manned jointly by Phoenicians and Jews.[56] The Paraiba text reflects Phoenician-Jewish partnership at sea in the interim: four centuries after Solomon and one century before Herodotus.

In 1968 the antiquity of the Paraiba inscription was proved by the plaintext whose peculiarities were first duplicated in other Northwest Semitic documents excavated long after 1872. This proof did not explain all of the oddities, more of which are cleared up for the first time in this book through the requirements of the acrostic-telestic. The vowel letter W in ^{C}LYWNM (line 2) and ^{C}LYWNT (lines 3, 8) is necessary in order to indicate the letters needed for the acrostic letter in line 3 (N) and the telestic letters in line 2 (W) and line 8 (again W). In line 8, the telestic letter W is indeed the W of ^{C}LYWNT itself! The cryptogram would break down without the vowel letter W in lines 2, 3, and 8.[57]

The option to omit or include vowel letters was at the disposal of any scribe in 531 B.C. in accordance with the usages of the recent or remote past. This option provided our scribe with the orthographic flexibility he needed for constructing the acrostic-telestic within a plaintext.

The correctness of WL' NH (line 6) "we were not" is brought out by the same (hitherto unrecognized) construction in Job 23:11, as noted above. Scholars who failed to grasp the construction have emended WL' NH to WL' NHYH. Their emendation is ruled out by the numerical indicator (M = 13) which requires T for the acrostic letter in line 6.[58] This precludes the addition of the two letters (YH) which would throw the count off.

The vowel letter Y in KY (line 7) is needed to make the indicator (M = 13) point to the needed aleph as the telestic letter. In the telestic message K is written without –Y because there is no room for a ninth letter in a message limited to eight letters—one letter from each of the eight lines in the plaintext.

Now that we have solved the acrostic-telestic, we see why the text is correct as it stands, and why the emendations as those above are untenable.

Unlike the Norse scribes who, as we shall have occasion to note, often make intentional mistakes in spelling and in grammar for the sake of their cryptograms, the Paraiba scribe, as far as we can tell, never deviates from existing usages.[59]

ADDENDUM

As soon as I communicated my solution of the acrostic-telestic in the Paraiba inscription to Alf Mongé, he began to search for the secret to its key (1–2–8–3–7–5–4–6). The fact that it begins with 1–2 suggests that concealment for its own sake was not the overriding consideration. There must be a special reason for the sequence 1–2–8–3–7–5–4–6.

Mongé sought a geometric pattern. His experience with runic cryptograms had brought him to the realization that the Norse puzzlemasters sometimes operated with geometric patterns based on different kinds of Christian crosses. The Yahwistic character of the Paraiba puzzlemaster led Mongé to look for a

Jewish geometric pattern, the most familiar being the six-pointed Star of David, composed of two triangles. So Mongé arranged the numbers 1 to 8 thus:

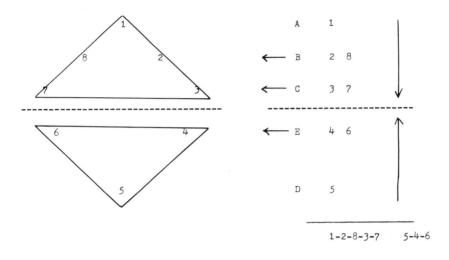

The upper triangle, if we read down from the point, and from right to left on each line (which is the Hebrew direction of writing), gives us 1 + 2 + 8 + 3 + 7 = 21, regarded as the regnal year of Hiram III when the voyage ended upon disembarking in the New World. The plaintext tells that the crew embarked in the 19th year of Hiram and sailed for 2 years. Though Hiram reigned only 20 years, the sailors at sea had no means of knowing that he was no longer on the throne 2 years later.

The lower triangle, if read up from the point, and then from right to left, yields 5 + 4 + 6 = 15, which is the number of people who reached their destination and disembarked. The plaintext states that the 15 were 12 men and 3 women.

There is a tradition that the wonder-working King Solomon operated with an eight-pointed star (E. A. Wallis Budge, *Amulets and Talismans,* Collier Books Edition, Macmillan, New York, 1970, p. 281; and *The Book of Charms and Talismans* by

"Sepharial," no date, p. 62, which Mongé tells me mentions all sorts of different geometric figures built around King Solomon's eight-pointed star). This suggests a geometric pattern as follows:

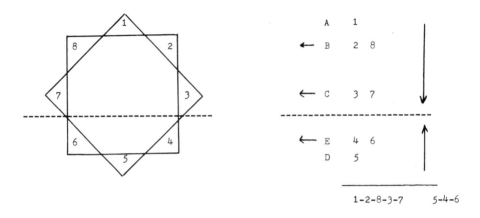

Since we do not possess the puzzlemaster's work sheets, we are ignorant of exactly how he worked out his problem. But Mongé shows us how it could have been achieved, and has opened our eyes to geometric-pattern cryptograms, with an acumen that es-establishes a model for the rest of us. (See Schalit 1973, figure 76, for the eight-pointed star on a coin of the Jewish King Jannaeus Alexander.)

CHAPTER IV

The Vinland Map

The Vinland Map, now in the Yale University Library, was published in Skelton-Marston-Painter 1965. There are Latin legends on a world map that includes Vinland. The writing material and paleography point to a date around A.D. 1440, and to an Upper Rhine location such as Basel as the place where it was inscribed. The Latin legend #67 is an eight-and-a-fraction line composition attributing a mission to Vinland under the leadership of Bishop Henricus (whose native Scandinavian name is Eirikr Gnupsson) in the last year of Pope Paschal II (A.D. 1099–1118). Certain statements in this composition are problematic: for example, it makes Bjarni and Leif Erikson sailing companions[60] on the initial Viking discovery of Vinland (generally dated around A.D. 1003). Icelandic sources state that around 986 Bjarni had sighted Vinland but did not land. Afterwards, in Greenland, Leif Erikson bought his ship and sailed without him to Vinland, at the head of the first Viking expedition to land on continental American soil. Henricus, writing over a century later, could well have made some historical errors concerning the days of Leif Erikson.

Scholars disagree on the authorship and authenticity of the Vinland Map.[61] Some hold that it is a fifteenth-century pseudepigraphon that drew on earlier literary and cartographic sources, without any real connection with Norse expeditions to the New World, nor specifically with Henricus who lived in the twelfth century. Some suspect it is a nineteenth- or twentieth-century forgery.[62] Others believe that the Vinland Map reflects the actual explorations and cartography of Henricus in Vinland effected during the first quarter of the twelfth century.[63] There may well be a core of twelfth-century data, modified and embroidered in the course of transmission between the time of Henricus and of the scribe who prepared the Yale copy around A.D. 1440.

As the first bishop in America, Henricus is noteworthy. However, our main concern with the Vinland Map is the acrostic-telestic which happens to be in the same general tradition as the Paraiba text. The Vinland Map is couched in Latin which is the main channel of transmission of culture from the ancient Near East to Western Christendom.

In the text and translation of the Vinland Map legend, the acrostic and telestic letters are underlined in the Latin for the convenience of the reader. The cryptographic key is provided by the number of words on each line (for unlike the Paraiba inscription, each word is written separately).

Line   Key
1) Volente deo post longū iter ab insula Gronelanda per meridiem ad   (11

2) reliquas extremas partes occidentalis occeani maris iter facientes ad   (9

3) austrū inter glacies byarnus et leiphus erissonius socij terram nouam uberrimā   (11

4) videlicet vinifera inuenerunt quam Vinilandā insulā appelauerunt. Henricus   (8

5) Gronelande regionumq finitimarū sedis apostolicae episcopus legatus in hac terra   (10

THE VINLAND MAP

This map of the world is a copy made around A.D. 1440. Oddly enough, Iceland and especially Greenland are more realistically charted than Scandinavia. Greenland is, with a remarkable degree of accuracy, represented as an island, whereas modern cartography erroneously portrayed it as a peninsula jutting south from an Arctic continént of ice, until the nineteenth century.

The main text of Henricus (Latin legend "#67") is in the upper left corner.

Less accurate, but not less interesting, than Greenland is Vinland west of the Atlantic (called "Mare Occeanum" on the Map). This map of Vinland by Henricus together with his chart of the "HOOP" neighborhood (on Spirit Pond Runestone #1) reflects two levels of Old Norse cartography. Maps of vast regions incorporated data from charts of the component areas (even as this world map combines the maps of Vinland and of the Tartar Relation). Norse cartographers like Henricus made charts of localities like "HOOP" which they could use in formulating maps of whole countries like Vinland. In mapping Vinland, Henricus (or his school) indulged in considerable guesswork where knowledge was lacking. For Greenland, on the other hand, sufficient exploration and charting had laid the foundation for an excellent map. In the centuries of Erik the Red and of Bishop Henricus, the Arctic enjoyed milder temperatures than now, so that the circumnavigation of Greenland was feasible. Even so, it is greatly to the credit of the Norse Greenlanders and their Eskimo informants and partners that they charted the segments of the entire long coast of Greenland sufficiently for mapping the island as a whole. (Reproduced by permission of Yale University Press from *The Vinland Map and the Tartar Relation*, by R. A. Skelton, Thomas E. Marston, and George D. Painter. Copyright © 1965 by Yale University.)

Wintlandia Insula
a Brauno repa
et lecuho socijs

Mare Occeanum

Magne
Insule
Beati Brandani
Brandie
ꝓre

Desiderate
insule

Mare Occeanum

Hispanora

Beata insule
fortune

LEGEND "#67" ON THE VINLAND MAP
Bishop Henricus built his acrostic-telestic into this Latin text concerning his mission in Vinland.

6) spaciosa vero et opulentissima in postmo anno p. ss. nrj.
   Pascali accessit in nomine dei   (15
7) omnipotētis longo tempore mansit estiuo et brumali postea
   versus Gronelādā redit   (11
8) ad orientem hiemalē deinde humillima obediencia superiori
   vo-   (8
9) lūtati processit.

The English translation is:
1) By God's will, after a long voyage from the island of Greenland to the south toward
2) the farthest remaining parts of the western ocean sea,
   sailing
3) to the south amid ice, Bjarni and Leif Erikson as companions discovered a new land, most fertile
4) and even bearing vines, which island they named Vinland.
   Henricus,
5) the legate of the Apostolic See and bishop of Greenland and
   the neighboring regions,
6) arrived in this really spacious and most opulent land in the
   last year of our most Holy Father Paschal (= 1117-8) in the
   name of God
7) Almighty. He remained a long time summer and winter.
   Later he returned toward Greenland
8) northeastward and then in the most humble obedience to the
   will of his superiors
9) proceeded (back to Europe?).

The acrostic letters are:

P	E	R	E	E	O	S	T
1	2	3	4	5	6	7	8

and the telestic letters are:

R	C	U	H	I	S	N	E
1	2	3	4	5	6	7	8

Alf Mongé perceived that RCUHISNE is an anagram for HENRICUS who is named in line 4 of the plaintext. To get this reading, the order 1-2-3-4-5-6-7-8 must be changed to 4-8-7-1-5-2-3-6 = the key sequence which must be applied to both the acrostic and telestic, so that we obtain:

acrostic	E	T	S	P	E	E	R	O
key	4	8	7	1	5	2	3	6
telestic	H	E	N	R	I	C	U	S

The acrostic *et spe ero* "and in hope I shall be" is idiomatic for "I shall live in hope." The Latin idiom (*spe esse*) has the same meaning as the verb in the Paraiba telestic for declaring the author's religious faith.

When Mongé made his discovery, the acrostic-telestics of Khorsabad and Paraiba had not yet been surmised, let alone solved. He therefore had no means of knowing that the Vinland Map type of acrostic-telestic was not of Norse origin, for it appears in the Paraiba inscription of the sixth century B.C., while the content of the Vinland Map acrostic-telestic (author's name and formulation of faith) occurs on the Khorsabad tablet of the eighth century B.C.

We have followed the Latin text as originally published by R. A. Skelton (Skelton-Marston-Painter 1965, p. 140) with one correction: *Gronelādā* (instead of Skelton's *Gronelandā* in line 7). Armando Cortesão (in Washburn 1971, p. 16) correctly observed that in line 7 (and on the map of Greenland itself), the name of the island ends in *-lāda* (not *-landa* as in lines 1, 5).[64] Though Cortesão did not realize it, the omission of this *n* in line 7 is necessary for the indicator ("11") to designate the right telestic letter: "n" in "Gronelādā redit" is the eleventh letter from the end only if *-lādā* is read instead of *-landā* here. The other part of Cortesão's observation is harder to explain. He notes that in both line 7 and on the map of Greenland, the name of the island is spelled "Grouelāda" with *u* instead of *n*. While *u* and *n* look somewhat alike, they can nevertheless be distinguished in the handwriting of the scribe. It would not be surprising if this repeated misspelling turns out to be intentional, for a reason (cryptographic?) yet to be discovered.

That "8" is the cryptographic key for line 8 in both the Paraiba and Vinland Map texts, need not be accidental. This use of "8" should be compared with the alphabetic acrostic in Psalm 119 which opens (as we have already noted) with 8 verses beginning with aleph (the first letter in the alphabet), then with 8 verses beginning with bet (the second letter of the alphabet), and so forth, until the Psalm ends with 8 verses beginning with tau (the last letter of the alphabet).

Cryptographers are familiar with a kind of "key" that serves as a mnemonic. What easily remembered name, word, or phrase could be used to remind us that the acrostic-telestic in the Vinland Map is to be unscrambled in 4-8-7-1-5-2-3-6 order? Alf Mongé suggests that LYSANDER, the name of the Spartan general, naval commander, and statesman (died 395 B.C.), is the mnemonic key. The letter in LYSANDER that occurs first in the alphabet is A to which we shall assign the number "1"; the letter in LYSANDER that occurs next in the alphabet is D = "2"; then comes E = "3"; and so forth with L = "4," N = "5," R = "6," S = "7," and Y = "8." Thus the name provides the key for rearranging the letters in the acrostic and telestic:

L	Y	S	A	N	D	E	R
4	8	7	1	5	2	3	6

It is hard to find in any language another eight-letter name, word, or phrase that provides this sequence. Mathematical probability favors Mongé's proposal. But why the name of Lysander? Like Henricus, Lysander was a leader with an impressive naval record. Both men were recalled by their superiors from a distant assignment. Moreover LYSANDER is an appropriate key because Lysander was recalled by an enciphered order as we have already observed.

Henricus and every educated priest in the Latin tradition had access to the history of Lysander including his recall by crypto-gram, in the Latin translation of Plutarch's *Lives*. This would not only explain why LYSANDER was chosen as the key, but also reflect the channel of transmission from Greece to Rome of the art of encipherment within the matrix of general culture.

The Paraiba acrostic-telestic unscrambles in 1-2-8-3-7-5-4-6 order. Conceivably some eight-letter Canaanite name, word, or phrase served as the mnemonic key. In any case, we have discov-ered so much cryptographic continuity, from the ancient Near East to Medieval Europe, that it would be worth searching for the Paraiba counterpart of LYSANDER in the Vinland Map.

The Vinland Map with its intricate acrostic-telestic is hardly a translation, but rather an original composition in Latin. The Vin-land Map bridges the gap between the ancient Near East and Scandinavia, via Latin Christianity.

The "blunders" in the Vinland Map have been pointed out by classicists and other scholars. In line 6, *Pascali* is a wrong geni-tive of *Pascalis,* which should end in -*is* in the genitive as well as nominative. In line 5, *in* is the wrong preposition to be used with *accessit* (line 6), but this "error" can be explained because the *i* of *in* is the telestic letter needed to supply the *i* of "Henricus." Also in line 5, *(episcopus) Gronelande* "(bishop) of Greenland" is acceptable as a genitive in -*e*, but it would be more classical and consistent if the suffix -*ae* had been used as in *apostolicae* in the same line. Here again, the cryptogram explains the genitive suffix -*e* instead of -*ae*; the -*e* is required by the acrostic. Had *Gronelandae* been written, the key (= 10) would have pointed to the wrong letter (*a*). Instead of deploring such "errors," we should see whether they are the result of cryptograms.

The *Proceedings of the Vinland Map Conference* held in Washington, D.C., 15–16 November 1966, has been published (Washburn 1971). It is an informative set of papers and discussions by specialists in various component fields. While some of the skepticism is to be expected, there is also some gratuitous denigration and ridicule. Careful scholarship, particularly on the part of Skelton, who was responsible for the Vinland Map part of the Yale publication (Skelton-Marston-Painter 1965), had provided good reasons for attributing the parchment, script, etc., to the Upper Rhine (perhaps Basel) around A.D. 1440. Robert S. Lopez casts aspersions on the authenticity of the Vinland Map by stating (p. 31): "It is not beyond the power of a good paleographer to imitate perfectly any medieval handwriting on blank sheets of genuinely old parchment and with ink freshly made from a medieval recipe. Such ink cannot be artificially aged on paper, but the Vinland Map is on parchment, where fresh ink can look old if it is skillfully discolored." Lopez's suspicion duplicates Clermont-Ganneau's false solution of the Shapira "forgeries." Instead of realizing that Shapira's texts on parchment were genuine, Clermont-Ganneau "proved" that Shapira had faked the writing on old parchment. Indeed he did Lopez "one better": he told exactly how and from what kind of supply Shapira had procured the parchment. A brilliant piece of detective work, except that it was totally wrong.[65]

Lopez (pp. 31–32) goes on to inform us that it is quite easy "to produce wormholes with a hot wire or with live worms." Indeed he has "heard from reliable sources of an English antiquarian who has a stable of live worms." Since we live in a world of forgers who are supplied with ancient parchment, make ink from medieval recipes, and keep stables of live worms, we shall presently test the authenticity of the Vinland Map by criteria beyond any forger's capability for good or evil; to wit, *subsequent* discoveries.

Lopez, unlike some other skeptics at the Conference, believes that the hypothetical forgery was perpetrated quite recently: "Were it possible to question the unidentified seller, we might perhaps bring back the counterfeiter, alive or dead—but probably alive."

Stephan Kuttner is inclined to accept the manuscript as a

document copied around A.D. 1440, but rejects any real historic connection with the activities of Henricus in the twelfth century. He concludes that "it is a piece of hagiographic composition, done before or in the fifteenth century, for the first bishop of Greenland" (p. 113), Henricus. And yet even Kuttner has been bothered by serious doubts, because in 1895, Luka Jelič, without citing any source, refers to Eirikr Gnupsson as the bishop of Greenland *"regionumque finitimarum"* ("and the neighboring regions") using the same words as the Vinland Map legend. Kuttner observes (p. 112): "One gets an uneasy feeling when one has to consider the possibility that the mapmaker might have read Luka Jelič's paper and borrowed the term *regionumque finitimarum* from him." It is hard to understand why Kuttner does not also consider the alternate possibility that if Jelič was not using some source yet to be discovered, he may have had access to our Vinland Map.

Cartographically, the Vinland Map is striking because it outlines Greenland realistically, including its north shore, as no other premodern map does. As Gwyn Jones puts it: "while the delineation of Vinland owes everything, or almost everything, to tradition, the delineation of Greenland appears to owe everything, or nearly everything, to first-hand knowledge" (p. 126). From about A.D. 900 to 1200 the Arctic went through a warmer period than later (see pp. 85, 128), when the sea ice made it virtually impossible for anyone to navigate around the north coast, even in summer. This suggests that all of Greenland was mapped not later than the twelfth century when Henricus was active in voyaging and mapmaking.

Ib Rønne Kejlbo is among those who feel that the Norse voyages were of importance for mapping the Atlantic and paving the way for Columbus's rediscovery of America in 1492 (p. 83). Or, as Erik Wahlgren puts it: between the eleventh century "and 1440, some more precise ideas about the northern reaches of the New World than those possessed by Adam of Bremen had become part of Latin learning" (p. 135).

Since the Vinland Map legend tells us that Henricus returned from Vinland and Greenland to his Roman superiors, Einar Haugen is rightly inclined to "accept the authenticity of the Vinland Map and to maintain that it furnishes precious additional and independent evidence of the Norse discovery." It is indeed "a reflection of information conveyed to Rome by [Eirikr] Gnupsson in the early part of the twelfth century" (p. 142). Haugen's conclusions are substantiated by developments that emerged after the 1966 Conference; namely, Henricus's Spirit Pond Runestones (which include the map of a Vinland locality) discovered in 1971.[66]

The cryptogram of Henricus in the Vinland Map adds a new dimension to the subject. The "bad Latin" is sometimes intentional for the sake of the acrostic-telestic, as we have noted. Otherwise, it is understandable as the composition of a foreigner in Rome from the far north. Whatever he lacked as a Latin stylist, he made up in talent as puzzlemaster in the best Norse tradition.

It is fortunate that the recognition of the acrostic-telestic and the discovery of the Spirit Pond Runestones came *after* the publication of the Vinland Map, thereby confirming its authenticity. It is *subsequent* discoveries that have validated some of the most unbelievable finds: the Shapira Scrolls, the Paraiba Stone, and the Vinland Map—to mention only a few of those found under "mysterious" conditions.

CHAPTER V

The Kensington Stela

Understanding and evaluating old documents such as runic inscriptions must be methodical if the results are to have any objective value. The first step is the establishment of what was actually written by the scribe. This normally takes the form of a facsimile accompanied by the clearest possible photograph of the original. The drawing of the facsimile is not purely mechanical, for it already contains elements of interpretation. To take an English illustration: A faint or questionable dot may give rise, in a handwritten document, to reading a problematic letter as either "e" or "i." One copyist may read "pen" while another prefers to read "pin." This kind of variation may cause major differences of interpretation. Knowledge and judgment, as well as sharpness of vision and steadiness of hand, affect the reliability of facsimiles.

The next step is transliteration into printed characters, preferably Latin letters. This stage further affects the interpretation. In the Paraiba inscription, the division into words is introduced at this point, and sometimes there is more than one possibility. ("Lighthouse keeping" is not the same as "light housekeeping".) In the Kensington Stela, words are separated by a special symbol (two vertical dots, like a colon), relieving us of that re-

sponsibility. However, there are other problems in the runic
script. Some letters are polyphonous: standing for more than one
sound. For instance, the letter normally standing for *th* (as in
"thing") also stands for *d* in the Kensington Stela. Translitera-
ting it as "D" is the most convenient way of rendering the runic
symbol[67] (because "TH" could be mistaken for the two runic
signs "T" and "H").

The next step is to translate the runic text from Scandinavian
into English. This not only poses difficulties of vocabulary and
grammar but requires a realistic appraisal of the historic circumstances under which the text was composed. Translating a
modern Icelandic newspaper article into English is accordingly a
much simpler task than translating the Kensington Stela. The
latter is not very difficult from the standpoint of verbal meaning,
but rather of historic setting. When we stand on the threshold of
new chapters in man's past, the significance of a text may run far
deeper than the literal translation. The Norse expedition that be-
queathed to us the Kensington Stela describes its mission as
opdagelsefard "a journey of discovery" (line 2). It is easier to
translate the word than to grasp the historic reality that those
Scandinavians risked their lives far from home, not primarily for
plunder, for trade, or for converting Indians to Roman Catholicism, but because their curious minds and restless spirits impelled them to explore and discover the unknown.[68]

Then comes the commentary on the plain meaning of the text.
For example, the first line states that the expedition included
Goths and Norsemen (forerunners of the Swedes and Norwegians respectively). This mixed background should prepare us for
dialect mixture in the text. Swedes and Norwegians can still
understand each other without studying each others' dialects. In
1362 when the Kensington Stela was inscribed, the two sets of
dialects ("Swedish" and "Norwegian") were much closer than
today.

Finally come the hidden messages, if the text happens to em-
body cryptograms. It takes considerable care on the part of a

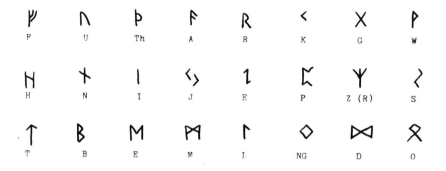

THE OLD 24-RUNE ALPHABET
(From Krause 1943, p. 7; for variants see Gordon 1957, p. 181)

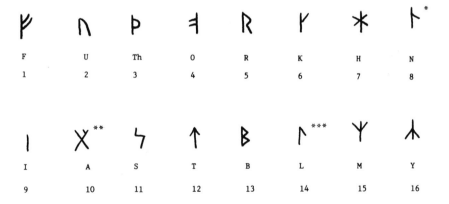

THE YOUNGER 16-RUNE ALPHABET
AS IT APPEARS IN THE SPIRIT POND RUNESTONES
(with numerical values)

*SP-3 uses ✝ .

**This atypical form is used in the SP and Kensington Runestones.

***Sometimes L follows M. The above order is required in SP where L = 14 crypto-graphically.

scribe to conceal cryptograms beneath a smooth plaintext. If the cryptograms are embedded in gibberish (like the Spirit Pond texts), much less skill is required. But the Paraiba and Kensington inscriptions are so easily translatable as plaintext that no one, until quite recently, suspected the presence of cryptograms beneath the plaintext. Needless to say, just as plaintext must be demonstrable linguistically, hidden meanings must be demonstrable cryptographically.[69]

The first runes appeared in Denmark and Norway around A.D. 200 and continued to be written in Scandinavia until early modern times. Up to about A.D. 800 the runic alphabet comprised 24 letters, when at that time a shorter runic alphabet of 16 letters appeared in Denmark and gradually spread throughout Scandinavia and the Nordic colonies in Russia, the British Isles, the Faeroe Islands, Iceland, Greenland, and North America. The reduction from 24 to 16 letters necessitated further polyphony, but the economy in the number of letters was evidently welcome, for the shorter runic alphabet prevailed.

Runic script is an offshoot of the familiar alphabet, even though few of the runic letters retain the same shape and sound of the older forms found in the ancient Mediterranean. In the runic signs in the texts covered in this book, "I" and "R" are essentially the same in appearance and sound as in the Latin alphabet. (The "F" rune is also related in form and sound to Latin "F.") Unlike the Ugaritic, Phoenician, Greek, and Latin forms of the alphabet, which retain much of the original sequence of letters, the runic alphabet is listed quite differently. Thus the six opening letters are F-U-TH-A-R-K so that a runic alphabet is known as a "futhark." This drastic rearrangement of the letters reflects the gap between the futharks vis-à-vis the older Mediterranean forms of the alphabet.

The detailed origins of the early 24-letter futhark are so complicated that they have given rise to a variety of theories. An illustration of what we have to reckon with is the letter ◇ (variant: ○) which is a form of the Phoenician-Hebrew letter ^{c}ayin

(O, variant: ◇). Its Norse pronunciation is *ng* (as in "thing"), which is the way Hebrew ^{c}*ayin* is pronounced in the Spanish and Portuguese synagogue tradition. (Thus ŠM^c YŚR'L "Hear, O Israel!" in that tradition is pronounced *š^{e}mang yiśrā'ēl,* instead of the familiar non-Iberian *š^{e}ma^c yiśrā'ēl.* This value of ^{c}*ayin* seems to have affected a couple of the Ashkenazic and Yiddish pronunciations of Y^{c}QB "Jacob" (to wit, *Yankov* and its diminutive *Yankel*). It is not surprising to find a specifically Iberian feature in the early Mediterranean impact on Scandinavia.

The alphabet meant more to the ancients than to us. For them it was a number system as well as a means of spelling phonetically. We have seen how the Hebrews and Greeks used the letters for expressing numbers. When we examine the cryptograms in the Spirit Pond Runestones, we shall see that the Norse also associated the runes of their futharks with numbers.

There is a totally unnecessary controversy of long standing about whether or not runic writing had mystical or magic aspects for the runemasters and their Norse public. From the beginning the letters of the alphabet were viewed with awe and regarded as fraught with magic and mystery. The derivation of the very word "rune" shows that it is in the tradition of the mystery-laden Mediterranean alphabet.[70]

There is no substitute for knowing the linguistic and graphic facts of runology. Making rules as we go along, in blissful disregard of the established body of knowledge, would serve no useful purpose.

All dialects are subject to changes that go with differences in time, place, and social milieu. The first runic inscriptions (from about A.D. 200–550) are in Early Scandinavian which had not yet diverged significantly from its sister Teutonic languages. Later (about 550–1050) the dialects are grouped together as Common Scandinavian, which had still not diverged from each other into really different speech groups. Thereafter (around 1050–1350) we encounter slight but sufficient differences that enable scholars to distinguish Old Danish, Old Swedish, Old Norwegian, Old

Icelandic, etc. The dialects used in Norway and in the Scandinavian colonies to the west (Britain, the Faeroes, Iceland, Greenland, etc.) are called "Old Norse" (or "Old Icelandic" though
the latter is best restricted to the island of Iceland). By 1350 the
dialects had begun to turn into the modern Scandinavian languages, and that is why the Kensington Stela of 1362 has some
"modern" fourteenth-century features. The peculiarities of the
Stela are duplicated in other Scandinavian texts of the fourteenth century.[71]

The preceding paragraph implies that while we must be aware
of the rules, we must also be flexible when tackling new material. Who makes the rules and on what grounds? I happen to have
formulated the first comprehensive grammar of Ugaritic. Until
its first edition in 1940, the newly discovered tablets from Ugarit
were interpreted without any firm set of rules. So I scrutinized all
the available texts and formulated the rules. More material came
to light through continued excavation, and the book went
through a number of necessarily revised and greatly enlarged edi-
tions. Rules are man-made and must be used as aids rather than
worshiped as sacred cows. It is established that the Old World
runic texts from the Black Sea to Iceland have individual scribal
as well as chronological and local differences. Runestones from
Greenland, Vinland, or Minnesota cannot be expected to fit into
any prefabricated system that arbitrarily excludes North America from the "Runic World." The Minnesota and Maine runestones share certain features which we can provisionally call
"American," while they also differ from each other on account
of time, place, and scribal individuality.

The same holds for the futharks. The variations in Old World
rune-forms are numerous. The shapes of the runes from Maine
and Minnesota cannot be expected to fit in minute detail into any
prior arbitrary scheme, any more than the Old World runic
forms on which various charts have been successively based. The
runestones from Maine and Minnesota share an otherwise un-
common form of "A," but they differ in other respects, separated as they are by a thousand miles and two and a half centuries.

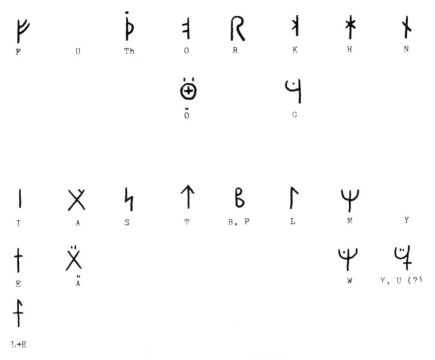

THE KENSINGTON RUNES

The Kensington Stela, like the Paraiba Inscription, is demonstrably authentic on two counts: (1) peculiarities of the plaintext have been confirmed in other fourteenth-century runic inscriptions that became known only after 1898 when the Stela was found, and (2) its cryptograms have proved to be genuine by developments that unfolded more than half a century after 1898. Accordingly, any difficulties that remain are not grounds for suspicion, but rather work to be done.

The Stela was erected in 1362, only 130 years before Columbus's first voyage to America. Possibly Norse reports about Vinland had reached Columbus and affected his thinking and plans.[72] The Norse achievement preceded, and maybe helped pave the way for, the Columbian Age of Discovery. Columbus claims to have sailed to Iceland in 1477, long before his epoch-making voyage of 1492. In any event Roman Catholic Europe knew of the Viking voyages celebrated in Scandinavian literature and known to the Vatican with Latin documentation.

The Black Plague (1349–50) may have been a factor in slowing the Scandinavians' drive to go on with the exploration and colonization of North America. Even their Greenland colonies neared exhaustion in the fourteenth century, during which the last dated American runestone was inscribed in Minnesota in 1362.

The following is the transliteration of the Kensington Stela:

obverse
1) 8 : GÖTER : OK : 22 : NORRMEN : PO :
2)   I : OPDAGELSEFARD : FRO :
3)   WINLAND : OF : WEST : WI :
4) HADE : LÄGER : WED : 2 : SKLEAR : EN :
5) DAGS : RISE : NORR : FRO : DENO : STEN :
6) WE : WAR : OK : FISKE : EN : DAGH : ÄPTIR :
7) WI : KOM : HEM : FAN : 10 : MAN : RÖDE :
8) AF : BLOD : OG : DED : A V M :
9)   FRÄELSE : AF : ILLU :

side
10) HAR : 10 : MANS : WE : HAWET : AT : SE :
11) APTÏR : WORE : SKIP : 14 : DAGH : RISE :
12)   FROM : DENO : ÖH : AHR : 1362

The translation is:
1) 8 Goths and 22 Norsemen on (a)
2)   journey of exploration from
3)   Vinland over (the) west. We
4) had (pitched) camp by 2 boat slips, one
5) day's travel north of this stone.
6) We were (out) and fished one day. After
7) we came home (we) found 10 men red
8) with blood and dead. Ave Virgo Maria!
9)   Save (us) from evil!
10) (We) have 10 men by the sea to look
11) after our ship(s) 14 days travel
12)   from this island. Year 1362.

Line 1 indicates that the expedition was staffed by Swedes (Goths) and Norwegians (Norsemen).

Lines 2 and 3 inform us that the expedition started in Vinland, along the Atlantic seaboard, and proceeded to what is now central Minnesota.

The Stela, weighing over two hundred pounds, was not intended to be moved. Accordingly the location of "this stone" (line 5) is meant to be a fixed place, possibly near the spot where it was unearthed in 1898.

The expedition was Roman Catholic. The invocation to the Virgin Mary in line 8 and the use of Latin letters (A V M) were commonplace among the priests who constituted the literate class.

In line 8, OG ends in *g* which is voiced because it has undergone partial assimilation to the following word (DED) which begins with voiced *d*. Elsewhere the conjunction is OK (lines 1, 6) because it is followed by a voiceless consonant.

The word "island" (line 12) can refer to any land mass with a shore. In ancient Greek, the word for "island" can be applied to the most vast of continents.[73] The Hebrew *'îy,* Irish *hy,* Scandinavian *ö* (written ÖH here) all meaning "island" may owe its distribution to international mariners who spread the word from language to language. When sailors approach a shore, there is no way of knowing whether what they see is a large island or a continent.

The "10 men red with blood and dead" (lines 7-8) reminds us of the Paraiba text in which "10 died" marks the end of the cryptogram that confirms the plaintext date. Does this expression serve the same function in both texts?

Alf Mongé has noted that the indentations in the Kensington Stone mark off lines 1-3 as one section, and lines 4-9 as another. He also surmised that the pentathic numerals in these sections confirm the date 1362 whose digits total 12: For if we add

$$
\begin{array}{r}
1 \\
3 \\
6 \\
2 \\
\hline
\end{array}
$$

the total is   12

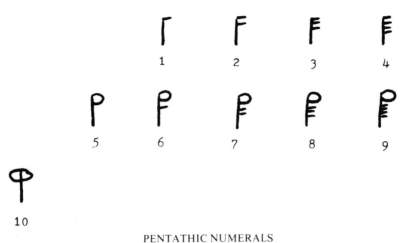

PENTATHIC NUMERALS

In the first section (lines 1–3), the 8 Goths and 22 Norsemen
have digits totaling 12:

$$8$$
$$2$$
$$2$$
_____

whose total is   12

In the second section (lines 4–9), the 2 boat slips and X
deadmen also total 12, for in the pentathic system of numbers,
ten is indicated not by "1" followed by "0," but by a single symbol. Accordingly we shall use Roman numerals for adding the
numbers of the boat slips and the deceased:

II   (boat slips)
X   (dead men)
_____

adding up to   XII

Here we have a cryptogram of $12 + 12 = 24$, which is twice $1 + 3 + 6 + 2 = 12$. Thus the date is confirmed by its double; and the final entry of "10 (dead)" indicates the conclusion of this particular date-cryptogram, as in the Paraiba text.

Since the numbers discussed above had to add up to a required total, some if not all of them may be contrived. There need not have been precisely 8 Goths and 22 Norsemen. Nor does the number of boat slips matter historically. And we have reason to believe that the "10 dead men" simply indicates that we have reached the end of the cryptogram that confirms the plaintext date by its double, as in the Paraiba Inscription.

The Stela contains other cryptograms worked out by Mongé to whom the reader is referred. It may be of interest, however, to note that the precise date of Sunday, 24 April 1362, is enciphered within the plaintext.[74]

CHAPTER VI

The Spirit Pond Runestones

The Kensington Stela provides its own date: 1362. The Vinland Map states that it is the work of Henricus, whose activity unfolded in the tens and twenties of the twelfth century. The Spirit Pond Runestones, however, confront us with a more difficult problem. Its plaintext dates of 1010 and 1011 refer back to earlier times. The name of Henricus and his date of 6 October 1123 that is commemorated, are enciphered and will probably seem confusing to scholars unfamiliar with such cryptograms. Before we attempt to interpret the Spirit Pond stones and place them in their proper setting, we must review briefly the history of Old Norse exploration and discovery in the Arctic and Atlantic oceans.

Icelandic literature and Vatican epistles provide a historic framework into which the runestones fit. There are also archaeological remains from all over the Viking world. An important excavation was conducted by Helge Ingstad at L'Anse aux Meadows near the northern tip of Newfoundland, where Viking houses and artifacts of roughly A.D. 1000 were unearthed.[75]

The pertinent parts of the two most significant Old Icelandic manuscripts along with several relevant Papal documents were conveniently published in 1906.[76] Syntheses of the Viking explorations in America have been written by many authors, including Haugen,[77] Holand,[78] and Pohl.[79]

The tale of Norse explorations in the Arctic can be traced back to about A.D. 870, when a Norseman named Ottar sailed from his native shores six days north, then four days east, and finally five days south to discover the populated mouth of a great river: presumably the Dvina in Russia. Ottar narrated his exploits to King Alfred the Great of England who added it to his translation of Orosius's *History of the World*.[80]

Shortly after Ottar's voyage, Harald the Fairhaired became King of all Norway in 872 and ruled for seventy-three years. By annulling the right to own land except by royal permission, he alienated so many proud farmers that thousands migrated to Iceland. Among the late emigrants to Iceland were Thorwald and his son Erik the Red around 950. Thorwald had been outlawed for manslaughter and fled by ship with his son. Together they sailed to Iceland with a few slaves and some cattle. Iceland had been discovered about a century earlier and all of the good land had been occupied. Thorwald and Erik went to the northwest corner of the island where the father died.

Erik married and was getting settled when strife and duels resulted in his being outlawed from his new home in Haukadal, in a more southern and desirable part of Iceland. Erik lost his farm and slaves but still had his ship. Further fighting and bloodshed led to his banishment, presumably for three years. He had heard tales of a Viking named Gunnbjorn, who around 930 (?) had been blown off course onto some skerries in the west. Since Erik needed a refuge, he sailed out that way with a small party and found Greenland. Thus the discovery of Iceland around 850 and Gunnbjorn's accidental finding of the skerries proved to be the stepping-stones for Erik's 982 discovery of Greenland, which lies in the Western Hemisphere.

The three years of banishment elapsed and Erik returned to Iceland in the fall of 985 to tell that he had found a new land larger than Iceland with room for thousands of settlers. The prospect of free land appealed to many Icelanders whose native island was overcrowded. Erik assured them that there were no aborigines to contend with (for the Eskimos did not pose any problem in Greenland till the thirteenth century). He also reported that hunting was much better than in Iceland, for Greenland had many seals, walruses, polar bears, and even whales. He had chosen his homestead and planned to return the following summer.

Erik called the great area he had discovered "Greenland" hoping to attract settlers by such an inviting name. He sailed back in the summer of 986 with 35 (or according to another tradition, 25) ships, but due to rough seas only 14 of the ships reached Greenland.

Erik's achievement is impressive in the annals of discovery. Because the eastern shore was so uninviting, he rounded the southern end of the island and explored the western coast of Greenland, naming many localities such as islands, headlands, and fjords. The extent of his explorations, covering a thousand miles, was not matched for 700 years. Six centuries passed before the Danish government tried to rediscover Greenland but it took another century of well-equipped expeditions to rediscover as much as Erik did in a single voyage.

The availability of large land grants eventually attracted more settlers so that the population grew to approximately two and a half or three thousand. The main development, where Erik made his home, is called the East Settlement. About two hundred miles northwest of it, near the site of modern Godthaab, was the smaller Western Settlement.

The foundations of Erik's large house at Eriksfjord still remain.[81] He died around 1004.

Meanwhile, in 999, Erik's son Leif, when only twenty years old, voyaged to Norway where he called on King Olaf, son of Trygve. Olaf, a devout Christian, so convinced Leif of the new religion that Leif and his men were converted. Leif's missionary zeal was the first step in a chain reaction that culminated in the conversion of Greenland to Roman Catholicism. Eventually Greenland had a large cathedral, quite a number of smaller churches, and the status of a bishopric destined to receive the attention of several Popes.

The two main literary sources for the Norse discovery and exploration of continental America are (1) The Flatey Book ("Flatey" means "Flat Island"), which reflects an essentially Greenland viewpoint and was compiled and copied by two priests in the latter part of the fourteenth century; and (2) Hauk's Book, which has an Icelandic point of view and was copied by an Icelandic scholar, Sir Hauk Erlendson, in the early part of the fourteenth century.

The Flatey Book narrates that Bjarni the son of Herjulf sailed to Eyrar, on the southwest coast of Iceland, where he expected to find his father. But it was the fall of 986, the year that Erik sailed with his party to Greenland. Bjarni, a determined man, was resolved to spend the winter with his father Herulf, who, as he learned at Eyrar, had accompanied Erik to Greenland. Although neither Bjarni nor any of his crew had ever been to Greenland, he gathered information about it and set sail to find his father.

Bjarni was blown off course into a fog by north winds for many days. When the sun finally appeared, he got his bearings from the sun by day and the stars by night, and eventually sighted a well-wooded land without mountains. He decided it did not correspond with the descriptions of Greenland, so he refused to land and sailed on for two days. Sighting a flat country covered with timber, he again refused to land because it could not be Greenland which he knew had large glaciers. So he headed out to sea before a southeast wind for three days when he sighted a third land which was high and mountainous with ice on it. He stayed on course and noted it was an island that could not be the vast Greenland. Again refusing to land, he sailed on for four more days whereupon they sighted another land which Bjarni said corresponded with what he had heard about Greenland. By evening they reached a cape with a boat on it. This was Herjulfsness (Herjulf's Cape) where his father dwelt.

The tale represents Bjarni as a man of single-minded determination and a remarkable navigator. Yet when he reported his experiences, he was blamed for his lack of curiosity because he failed to set foot on the three countries he had sighted. Instead of being hailed as a discoverer, he was held in some contempt. This reaction reflects the greatness of the Old Norsemen, who had the curiosity of true explorers. For them it was not enough for a captain to find his way back home. Exploring the unknown was a way of life, and throwing away an opportunity to do so was reprehensible.

Leif was endowed with far more natural curiosity than Bjarni. As a mariner, Leif had established an enviable record, for in 999 he had sailed from Greenland to Norway without stopping in Iceland. On returning to Greenland, having heard about Bjarni's voyage, he bought his ship and sailed away to explore the lands that Bjarni had only seen from afar. Leif embarked with thirty-five men including a southerner (i.e., a German) named Tyrker.

Leif's course was the reverse of Bjarni's. Leif first came to the last land that Bjarni, before reaching Greenland, had sighted. Leif named it Helluland ("Land of Flat Stone") for on going ashore, he found glaciers, but no grass, and the land between the sea and the glaciers was like one flat stone.

The next country he called Markland ("Woodland") for he found it wooded, low, and with wide stretches of white sand.

The third country he found excellent. His approach to it was by an island carpeted with dew-covered grass. Leif and his men went ashore, tasted the sweet dew and returned to their ship. They sailed westward between the island and a cape that projected north from the mainland. At low tide their ship became grounded and the eager crew hurried ashore where a river flowed out of a lake. When the tide came in, they rowed back to the ship and took it up the river into the lake where they cast anchor. They took their gear ashore, built shelters, decided to winter there, and accordingly constructed large houses. It was probably in 1003 that Leif Erikson landed in continental America and built the nucleus of what he hoped would be a permanent settlement.

The waters were full of the biggest salmon they had ever seen. There was enough fodder for their animals even through the winter. It was so far south that on the shortest day of the year the sun rose before *dagmala stad* (= 9 A.M. breakfast) and set after *eyktar stad* (= 3 P.M. dinner).[82]

After the houses were constructed, Leif divided his expedition into two companies: one to explore the country, the other to guard the camp. He instructed the explorers to stick together and return by evening. Tyrker was missing one evening and Leif went out with a searching party of a dozen men to find him. They soon came across Tyrker in high spirits, for he had found vines laden with grapes and had his fill. The abundance of grapevines led Leif to name the country Vinland ("Wine Land").[83]

In the spring, Leif and his men loaded the ship with timber and the afterboat with fruit, and sailed back toward Greenland.

En route Leif spied a skerry on which a ship had been wrecked and the passengers and crew stranded. Leif transported all fifteen survivors including the shipowner Thorer and his wife Gudrid, to Greenland. There he invited Thorer, Gudrid, and three of the men to live with him as his guests, while he found lodgings for the others. Subsequently, Leif retrieved Thorer's cargo from the skerry. The rescue of the fifteen people and the salvage of the cargo won for Leif the epithet of "Lucky" for Leif the Lucky had won thereby wealth and honor.

An epidemic that winter (ca. 1004) took the lives of Erik the Red, Thorer, and a large part of Thorer's men. Erik had won fame by discovering, exploring, and colonizing Greenland. Leif discovered and erected buildings in a much better place to live: Vinland. Moreover, Leif had dedicated himself to a spiritual ideal: the propagation of Christianity. (Erik lived and died a pagan.)

Leif's brother Thorwald felt that Leif had not explored Vinland sufficiently. So in Leif's ship, Thorwald sailed with thirty men to Leif's camp in Vinland. The ability of Vikings to find exact points on distant shores of newly discovered lands implies the art of cartography and the writing of logs on which to base future sailing directions.

After laying up their ship, Thorwald's party remained quiet for the winter and fished for food.[84] In the spring, Thorwald with part of his crew explored the coast westward in the afterboat. During the summer they sailed and explored to the east and north. On discovering fjords that led to a beautiful wooded headland that pleased Thorwald, he decided to build his house there. But trouble with the natives broke out, and Thorwald died from an arrow wound. He was buried with a cross at his head and feet on the spot he had chosen for his home.

His party returned to Leif's camp to spend the winter with the other members of the expedition. In the spring they returned in their ship laden with vine wood and fruit, to Greenland where they reported to Leif in Eriksfjord.

When Erik died (ca. 1004) Greenland had not yet been Christianized. By the end of Thorwald's expedition (ca. 1004–1007) Greenland was Roman Catholic.

Erik had another son, Thorstein, who had married the widowed Gudrid and set out to recover Thorwald's body for burial in the church built by his mother near Brattahlid in Greenland. His ill-starred voyage ended on the Western Settlement of Greenland where he died in an epidemic. Gudrid, in 1009, reached Brattahlid with Thorstein's body, and became Leif's ward.

That summer a wealthy and gifted guest arrived in Greenland: Thorfinn Karlsefni, the son of Thord. At Eriksfjord he fell in love with Gudrid and asked Leif for her hand in marriage. During the following merry winter with nuptials in Brattahlid, Karlsefni heard about Vinland. Hiring sixty men and five women, he organized his expedition.[85] They agreed to share evenly all the worldly goods they might gain in Vinland. Planning to stay there, they took along cattle. Karlsefni asked Leif for his houses in Vinland, but Leif, who hoped to return there, was willing only to lend, not give them. This account illustrates how Old Norse leaders like Leif were interested in establishing permanent settlements in America, and not merely in making occasional voyages.

Karlsefni sailed to Vinland and found Leif's booths in good condition. (Again we note the Vikings' ability to land at exact points on distant, recently discovered shores. This makes it likely that they had maps like the northwestern parts of the Vinland Map, and charts like the one on Spirit Pond Runestone #1.)

In Vinland, Karlsefni came to a river that ran into a lake, and then into the sea. It was possible to navigate into the river only at high tide because of sandbars outside the river mouth. Karlsefni sailed into the river mouth and named the area HOP (meaning "a small landlocked bay"). The Spirit Pond map (on SP-1) designates the findsite as HOOP, and it would be hard to find a place that better fits the description of Karlsefni's HOP.[86]

From a Greenlander's or even an Icelander's point of view, Vinland was a veritable paradise. Around HOP they found self-sown grain in the lowlands and grapes on the hills. The creeks were full of fish. They dug pits where land and sea met at high tide. At low tide there were halibut in the pits. The woods teemed with game.

After the first winter was over, they became aware of the natives. At last a troop of them emerged from the woods. A language barrier precluded verbal communication. The natives wanted to trade their packs and furs, particularly for weapons. Karlsefni refused to give weapons, and instead instructed the women to offer milk to the natives. The latter drank the milk and left their furs. The natives were also pleased with the red cloth that the Norsemen traded.

The ominous presence of the natives prompted Karlsefni to erect a strong pole fence for protection.

Gudrid bore a son to Karlsefni in Vinland. The boy, named Snorre, is the first known child born of European parents on American soil.

At the start of the second winter, a larger number of natives came to trade the same wares. This time Karlsefni told the women to carry out meat in exchange. The natives accepted this and presented their packs by throwing them over the fence. Unfortunately, one of Karlsefni's men killed a native who would have taken some weapons, and a battle soon followed. Though the natives fled, Karlsefni decided in the spring to return to Greenland with a cargo of vine wood, berries, and furs.

The time of Karlsefni's sojourn to Vinland (1010–1014) covers the plaintext dates (namely, 1010 and 1011) in Spirit Pond Runestones #1 and #3. This, along with the name HOOP on the map on SP-1, suggests that the Spirit Pond Runestones record an attempt at reactivating the settlement at HO(O)P that Karlsefni named early in the eleventh century.

The voyages of Bjarni, Leif, Thorwald, and Karlsefni were not forgotten in the North. Over a century after Thorfinn Karlsefni's expedition, Erik Gnupson (or more exactly, Eirikr Gnupsson), who had become Bishop Henricus of Greenland, sailed to Vinland in 1121 according to six Icelandic annals. In 1112 he had been appointed the first Bishop of Greenland by King Sigurd who had recently returned from a Crusade in the Holy Land.

The Vinland Map tells us that the diocese of Henricus embraced Greenland and the neighboring regions. His Vinland expedition indicates that his activities as bishop extended to continental North America as far south as Vinland. He was, as far as we know, the first Bishop in America. The Spirit Pond Runestones celebrate cryptographically the year 1123 in connection with Henricus's mission to Vinland. The Spirit Pond Map (on SP-1) ties in with the Vinland Map to confirm Henricus's interest in cartography.

The location of HOOP (= Thornfinn Karlsefni's HOP) on the
Spirit Pond map of part of Vinland suggests that Bishop Henricus's mission was to preserve the Christian devotion of the Nordic settlers who came in the wake of the settlement-minded sons
of Erik the Red and of Thorfinn Karlsefni.

Our records in Icelandic and Latin confirm the impression
conveyed by the American runestones that the Norsemen were
impelled to establish permanent Christian colonies in Vinland
and other parts of continental North America. Vatican archives
indicate the concern of the Church to preserve Christianity in the
north and west fringes of the known world. As a dedicated
bishop, Henricus was not merely interested in exploration and
map making, but in serving the Roman Catholic Church on one
of its most arduous and challenging frontiers. In this he was true
simultaneously to his Roman faith and Nordic tradition.

An intermittent series of papal letters deal with the far northwest.[87] On 13 February 1206 Pope Innocent III wrote to the
archbishop of Nidros, Norway, confirming the archbishop's
authority over the North Atlantic and Arctic islands including
the Orkneys, Faeroes, Iceland, Greenland, etc. Concern with the
Norsemen of Greenland implies involvement, directly or indi-
rectly, with the Greenlanders' chronic urge to colonize warmer,
richer, and more inviting areas farther south in continental
America.

On 4 December 1276 Pope John XXI wrote to the archbishop
of Nidros excusing him from personally visiting each and every
land for collecting tithes for the Holy Land, because the diocese
of Garda, Greenland, was so far. John instead advised him to
delegate reliable persons for supervising and collecting the tithe
in areas where it was impractical for the archbishop of Nidros to
visit in person. The pope also instructed the archbishop to convert into gold or silver the Greenlanders' payments in dairy products and fish, for they possessed no precious metal or currency.

On 31 January 1279 Pope Nicolas III granted the archbishop
of Nidros's request to be excused for lateness in collecting tithes

in Greenland, the island on which the city[88] of Garda was located, because the dangerous ocean voyage made sailing to Greenland quite infrequent. Nicolas authorized the archbishop to absolve clerics on Greenland and other islands in the same ocean, for tardiness in collecting tithes.

On 4 March 1282 Pope Martin IV answered the question of the archbishop of Nidros about what to do with the Greenland tithes paid in skins, tusks, and other arctic products. Martin instructed him to convert such wares into gold and silver for transmittal to Rome.

Thus the papal archives[89] reflect an abiding concern for the Roman Catholic community in Greenland. The East Settlement had twelve churches. The foundations of the large cathedral are still extant. The smaller West Settlement had four churches of which one fell into disuse.

The total Nordic population of Greenland was not large. The East Settlement may have had no more than 150 farms—many of them big—that supported about two thousand people. The West Settlement may have had only 75 farms with around four hundred people.[90] The roving spirit of the Greenlanders carried them (perhaps mainly on hunting expeditions) to distant and inhospitable islands off the west coast. Their presence there is attested by artifacts. An Eskimo employed by the Danish Naval Captain W. Graah in 1823–24, discovered on the offshore island of Kingigtorssuaq (a thousand miles north of the East Settlement!) three cairns. One of the cairns contained a runic inscription with the date 7 May 1244 according to Mongé.[91] Captain Graah was the first white man to reach so far north for centuries. The Kingigtorssuaq runestone shows that the Norsemen were penetrating remote areas in Greenland two and a half centuries after Erik discovered and colonized it.

The Eskimos began to pose problems for the Norse settlers of Greenland in the thirteenth century. They came into contact with the West Settlement and in 1342 occupied it; no Norsemen remained. The fact that no trace of bloodshed has been detected suggests that the West Settlement Norsemen may have migrated to a more desirable region: some perhaps southwestward to continental America which the Greenlanders had explored with repeated attempts at colonization.

One of the ironies of history is the failure of the Norse pioneers in America to make an impact sufficient to weld Europe and America into one permanently integrated ecumene. This, as we know, was destined for other West Europeans to the south, after Columbus's voyage in 1492. A contributing factor was the Black Plague which carried off between 25 and 35 percent of the Scandinavian population in 1349 and 1350. Yet that calamity did not terminate the Norse expeditions to America, as we shall observe. The chief reason for the failure of the Norsemen to conquer America was the hard fact that they lacked the firearms used by the Spaniards and other European colonists after 1492. While Norse weapons were superior to the Indians', they were not sufficiently better to compensate for the Indians' vastly greater numbers. Cortés and Pizarro with small numbers of men equipped with guns and horses quickly vanquished great Indian nations like the Aztecs and Incas. Any such Norse conquest was technologically impossible for Thorwald or Karlsefni.

King Magnus Erikson planned to force the Russians into accepting Roman Catholicism. In 1353 he managed to secure the necessary funding for a religious war, but news of the Plague then raging in Russia rendered any such plan suicidal. So instead, in 1354, he commissioned Paul Knutson to launch an expedition for the purpose of preventing Greenland from being lost to Christianity.[92]

There are other reports of Norse campaigns to Greenland in this period. Bishop Olaus Magnus wrote that King Haakon, who ruled from 1355 to 1380, conducted campaigns off the coast of Greenland.

Vatican records indicate a concern for Greenland into the fifteenth century. Pope Nicolas V, on 20 September 1448, wrote to the bishops of Shaoltensus and Olensus that thirty years earlier (= ca. 1418) the pagans (= Eskimos) devastated all except nine remote parochial churches in Greenland, enslaving the survivors. Some of the latter managed to return to the nine churches that had escaped destruction, but they were in dire want of food and were without priests to look after their needs. Nicolas asked the two bishops to see that qualified priests be sent, and rectors established to govern the restored parishes and churches and administer the sacraments. Nicolas also requested them to ordain some practical and able person as bishop in the name of the pope to conduct spiritual and temporal affairs. Thus less than half a century before Columbus's epoch-making voyage, Nicolas V was still concerned about Nordic Greenland as a bishopric.

Alexander VI (born 1431 and crowned Pope 11 August 1492) wrote to the church of Garda, Greenland, early in his reign. He mentions that no vessel was believed to have reached Greenland in eighty years (i.e., since the catastrophe of 1418?). Alexander stated that for eighty years no bishop or priest had governed the Greenland diocese in residence, and that the people must be lapsing into paganism. He described the church of Garda as being at the end of the earth in Greenland, where the inhabitants subsisted on dry fish and milk for want of bread, wine, and oil. Writing in the Age of Columbus, Pope Alexander VI sensed that the Norse settlements in Greenland were about to vanish and that the absentee bishops of Garda had only vestigial Christian communities in Greenland, whose Norse sailors had discovered, explored, and tried to establish permanent colonies in America from the early eleventh to the late fourteenth century. Dwindling remnants of the Norse may have survived in Greenland into the sixteenth century, but for all intents and purposes they vanished soon after 1500.

Norse activity in pre-Columbian America is confirmed by artifacts and inscriptions found from the northern tip of Newfoundland to central Minnesota, including the coast of Maine where three runestones were found by Walter Elliott on 27 May 1971 at Spirit Pond.

The three stones were found together and form an assemblage. Though they come fron one time (6 October 1123), they are not from one hand, for SP-3 is scribally distinct from the other two, as we shall observe. The map on SP-1 is a chart of the area around the find-site and suggests that the runestones were carved on the spot.

Why and how they were left at Spirit Pond are matters for speculation. Perhaps the party was threatened by natives and had to leave suddenly. Perhaps the stones were left in the hope that others would find them and get the message (such as sailing directions?). Such conjectures may run through our minds, but they are of little or no use in a historic investigation.

SPIRIT POND RUNESTONE #1:obverse

SP-1 is the most interesting of the texts and we shall start our discussion with the map on it. The area is, as we have noted, the vicinity of Spirit Pond where the stones were found. The find-spot itself is marked HOOP, which may well be Thorfinn Karlsefni's HOP.

The direction of the writing shows that the orientation of the map differs from modern usage which places north at the top. Matching the SP-1 map with a modern map of the area, indicates that the top is east, so that the arrow on the right is pointing south. Several of the topographical features can easily be equated with those on a modern map; e.g., Long Island (in the mouth of the Kennebec River), the heart-shaped Seguin Island in the estuary, and of course Spirit Pond and the Morse River.

Beneath HOOP, we read "UINLANT : 1011" meaning "Vinland (in the year) 1011." In the short (16-rune) alphabet as used in this text, "U" covers, *u, v,* and *w,* while "T" covers *d* as well as *t.* The date fits Thorfinn Karlsefni's expedition to Vinland.

On the right side we find:
TKA : TUA (U+L)
TAKH :
The first word, TKA is an anagram for TAK = *dag* "day" which is rewritten TAKH (*dagh* with final -H as in the Kensington Stela) directly beneath it. The second word is TUAU (with L combined with the final U to form a bindrune) cognate with Swedish *två,* English *two,* etc. To a Scandinavian speaking any dialect, *tuau dag* means "two days" regardless of grammatical or orthographic oddities. Accordingly the text suggests sailing directions as follows: "Sail in the direction of the arrow (= south) from HOOP (= Spirit Pond) for two days." Following the arrow brings one to Cape Cod. The voyage would take just about two days.

The final entry is (I+L) AK. Alf Mongé makes the acute observation that the two lines above (TKA : TUA (U+L) : TAKH

:) has eleven letters (for a bindrune counts as one letter). The runes have numerical values as follows:

F	U	Th	O	R	K	H	N	I	A	S	T	B	L	M	Y
1	2	3	4	5	6	7	8	9	10	11	12	13	14	15	16

The eleventh letter is S, which stands for "11," or conversely, "11" stands for "S." This is the runemaster's way of telling the initiated that (I+L)AK is preceded by S = SILAK, an anagram for SIKLA (*sigla*)[93] "sail(ed)." This provides the verb in the sailing direction and, as will be demonstrated below again and again, expresses the date 6 October 1123 cryptographically.

The first of the three lines has a significant numerical total:

$$
\begin{aligned}
T &= 12 \\
K &= 6 \\
A &= 10 \\
T &= 12 \\
U &= 2 \\
A &= 10 \\
U &= 2 \\
L &= 14
\end{aligned}
$$

total   68

Repeatedly throughout the Spirit Pond Runestones, we find totals of "34" and its double "68." Actually the three-letter TKA + the four-letter TUA (U+L) suggests "34." This impelled Mongé to conclude that Henricus's voyage took 34 days in one direction and 68 days for the round trip. However, this can hardly be right. How can anyone know in advance how long the return trip will require? Besides, a long voyage is not likely to take exactly the same time in each direction. Winds and currents affect speed, and they will be different coming and going. I am inclined to take a different approach. Just as the Kensington Stela date of 1362 is confirmed cryptographically by listing "12" items twice (for 1+3+6+2 = 12), the Spirit Pond date

$1+1+2+3 = 7$ is confirmed by "34" $(3+4 = 7)$ and "68" $(6+8 = 14 = $ twice 7). (We can trace the confirming of a date by its double, back to the Paraiba inscription of the sixth century B.C.) It was this feature of the Spirit Pond texts that first convinced me of the essential correctness of Mongé's solutions. At the time he did not know about the Paraiba confirmation of (year) "19" by enumerating "38" (= twice 19) items; nor had he approached the two examples of "12" in the Kensington Stela in this way. Accordingly, the correctness of his discovery cannot be assailed as "circular reasoning."

A normal person accustomed to dealing with plain language may ask why "day" is written twice: once anagrammed to TKA and once spelled TAKH on the next line, or why L is built into the last letter of TUAU "two" to form a bindrune, etc. The answer is that the runemaster gave the cryptograms priority over plaintext. By such oddities he managed to express "34," its double "68" and "11 = S" for his message: "Sail 2 days south from HOOP. (Dated in this memorable year of) 1123."

Mongé sees in the final word of the map side of SP-1, a cryptogram of the exact date to the day. Since $11 = S$, and there are 11 letters before $(L+I)$ AK, we can read $S(L+I)AK$. The runes have the following numerical values: $S = 11$, $(L+I) = 23$ (for $L = 14$ and $I = 9$), $A = 10$, and $K = 6$. The first two letters designate the year 1123, the next letter tells us that the month is the 10th = October, while the final letter designates the day of the month. Thus the date is 6 October 1123. This explains why SIKLA and its anagrams (SILKA, KILSA, and $S(L+I)AK$ appear repeatedly in the SP texts. They designate the all-important date.

The reverse side of SP-1 is also cryptographic. The eight-letter group MILTIAKI makes no convincing sense as plaintext. It could conceivably be interpreted as MILTI AKI *mildi Aki* "(O) generous Aki" for Aki is an Old Norse name that occurs in SP-3. But this is probably accidental. MILTIAKI might alternatively be an anagram for LITI A MIK (for *lit á mik*) "look at me" but

SPIRIT POND RUNESTONE #1:reverse

I question this, too. Any puzzling eight-letter group in these texts
may eventually prove to stand, through cryptographic manipulation, for "Henricus" which has eight letters.

Flanking the eight runes are two specimens of flora. On the left
is what looks like a vine with a cluster of grapes, while on the
right is a two-branched grain (or fruit) plant. The eight drawings
that follow are: a fish, a bird, a deer, a serpent (or eel), a native, a
man rowing a boat, an animal hide, and a bow and arrow. These
pictographs represent the flora, fauna, population, water trans-
portation, weapons, and products of Vinland. They may, however, also be intended to serve some cryptographic purpose.[94]
The vertical line with eight horizontals (the upper four crossing
it, and the lower four touching it on the right) suggests a cipher.
So too the "X" with an arc in the upper quadrant.

SP-2 can be transliterated without difficulty:

1) N(O+R)KSLOLK

2) S(L+I)A : K

The second line is an anagram for SIKLA "sailed" with the date "6 October 1123" inherent numerologically: S = 11, L+I = 23, A = 10, K = 6; i.e., year 1123, month 10, day 6.

Though the solution has not yet to my knowledge been found, the eight signs N-(O+R)-K-S-L-O-L-K suggest that they are some cryptic manipulation of the eight-letter name of Henricus.

SPIRIT POND RUNESTONE #2

SP-3 is the longest of the Spirit Pond texts, and one of the most extensive runic inscriptions found anywhere. It is sufficiently different from SP 1 and 2 to indicate that it was inscribed by another runemaster. Scribal lines are incised beneath each line of writing. The scribe usually writes ⊬ for N, which appears as ⊦ in SP 1 and 2. More significant is the use of Þ to cover Th and D, so that ↑ stands only for T in SP-3. In addition to bind-runes (monograms with a vertical stroke doing double duty: e.g., ⊹ E and ⌐ L fused into ⊬ L+E = L+I[95] in the 16-rune alphabet in which E and I fall together as I), there are other monograms composed of letters simply run together. Thus ⊬ = ⋈ IN, and ⊟ = ⊣⊣ OO. Some of the apparent monograms remain problematic. But the proof that the scribe occasionally runs signs together is ⋈ L+A in HA(L+A) DHIR in SP-3:15 = HALAD-HIR with the L and A well separated in SP-3:2.[96]

ᚼᛁᚥᚷ�13ᛅᛐ13ᚼᛅ �: ᚥ I ᚱᚼ ᚷ : ᚼᚠ ᚷ :
ᚱᛒ : ᚦ I ᚦ : ᛬ᚷ ᚱ ᚷ ᛒ ᛭ I ᚱ:ᛁ ᛒ ᚷ ᛡ ᛒ ᚷ ᚦ
᛭ ᚇ ᛁ : ᚷ ᛭ ᚱ : ᛩ ᛩ : ᛗ ᚇ ᚱ I ᚼ ᚷ ᚼ ᚇ ᛁᛐᚿ ᛁ :
ᚱ ᚠ : ᚱ I ᚼ I : ᚇ I ᚼ ᛏ : ᚱ ᚠ ᛬ᛐ ᛅ ᚱ: ᛩ ᛬ᚼ ᚷ ᚥ ᚷ ᛁ ᚠ
ᚇ ᛐ ᚥ : ᚼ ᚥ I ᛁ᛭ I ᛐ ᛁ ᚷ ᚷ ᛐ : ᛭ ᚷ ᚷ ᚥ ᛄ ᛐ᛬ᚥ ᚷ ᛐ :
᛭ ᚱ ᛡ I ᚥ ᛡᛐ: ᚷ ᛐ: ᚇ I ᚼ ᛏ ᛬ ᛒ ᚷ ᚷ ᚱ ᚷ ᚷ ᚥ ᚷ :
ᚼ I ᚥ ᚷ : ᚥ I ᚼ ᚼ ᚱ ᚱ I ᚥ ᛐ : ᛁ I ᛒ ᚷ ᛡ ᛒ ᚷ ᚦ ᛭
ᚇ ᛁ : ᚷ ᛭ ᚱ: ᛩ ᚱ ᚱ : ᚼ ᚥ ᚇ ᚷ ᚱ ᚷ ᚱ ᚠ ᚻ ᚼ ᚷ :
ᛒ ᚷ ᛁ ᚷ ᚱ ᚻ ᚱ ᛁ ᚷ ᛐ : ᛐ ᛭ ᚷ ᛐ ᛬
ᚼ I ᚥ ᚱ ᚷ ᚼ ᛭ I ᛒ I :

Another feature of SP-3 is the overlining of selected runes for cryptographic reasons, as will be brought out in the discussion.

A few of the signs, especially monograms, have not been identified with certainty. The questionable signs (indicated by inferior points or question marks) should be checked in the photographs and facsimiles. Here is the transliteration of SP-3:

obverse

1) SĪKAŦUMOÐIN : KILSA : S(L+I)Ā :

———————————————————————————

2) 17 : DID : HALADHIR : MIBAINBĀD-

———————————————————————————

3) HUM : AHR : 1010 : (?+?)ULISA SUIṬNK :

———————————————————————————

4) 12 : RISI : UIST : 12 : NOR : 10 : SAKAM(L+I)

———————————————————————————

5) UNK : SKIK̇HILMAN : HAAKON : FAN :

6) HR(I+N)IKIN : AT : UIST : BAALAAKA :

7) SILKA : KIYSLRIKN : MIBAINBADH-

8) UM : AHR : 1011 : SKUALAL(L+I) (O+O)SA :

9) BĀMAR̄ (O+O) RMAT : THAT :

10) SIKLĀSHIBI :

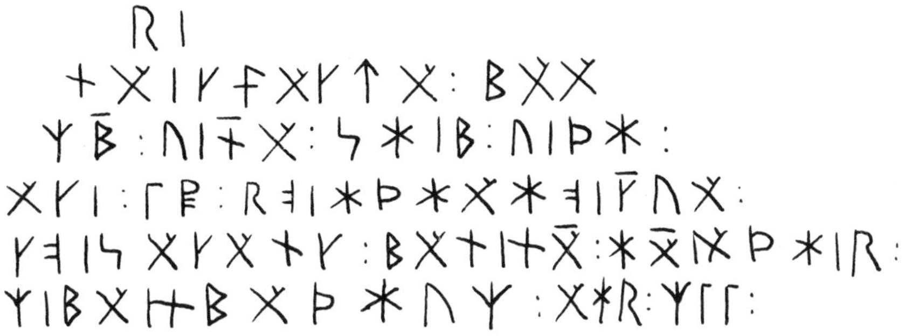

R I
+ X I Γ ꓧ X Ƭ ↑ X : B X X
Ƴ B̄ : �∩ I ꓧ X : Ϟ ⅋ I B : �∩ I Þ ⅋ :
X Ƴ I : Γ Ᏸ : R ꓺ ⅋ Þ ⅋ X ⅋ ꓺ Ϝ �∩ X :
Ƴ ꓺ I Ϟ X Ƴ X Ƭ Ƴ : B X Ƭ I Ƭ X̄ : ⅋ X̄ ꓜ Þ ⅋ I ꓣ :
Ƴ I ꓐ X Ƭ B X Þ ⅋ ∩ Ƴ : X ⅋ ꓣ : Ƴ Γ Γ :

SPIRIT POND RUNESTONE #3:reverse

reverse

11)] RI

12)] NAIK(L+I)AKTA : BAA-

13)] MB̄ : UIÑA : SHIB : UIDH :

_____

14) AKI : 17 : ROIHDHAHOIK̄UA :

_____

15) KOIŠAKANK : BANINĀ : HĀLADHIR :

_____

16) MIBAINBĀDHUM : AHR : ("M" 11 =) 1011:

_____

In line 16, "AHR M11" stands for "year 1011" with M =
1000 as in Latin, because here the "10" of "1011" is not to be
counted as a pentathic numeral in the following cryptogram:
   When we add all the pentathic numerals preceded by AHR
"year," we get a total of 34:

3)	10
3)	10
8)	10
8)	1
8)	1
16)	1
16)	1
total	34

This number (3+4 = 7) needed to confirm the date (1+1+2+3
= 7) would not come out right unless M (which is not a pentathic numeral) took the place of pentathic "10" in line 16.
   Now, when we add the other pentathic numerals (i.e., not preceded by AHR), we get a total of 68:

2)	10
2)	7
4)	10
4)	2
4)	10
4)	2
4)	10
14)	10
14)	7
	___
total	68

This total of 68 is twice the sum of the year numerals: $6+8 = 14$ ($=$ twice $1+1+2+3 = 7$).

When we add the numerical values of the letters overlined on line 1

letter	numerical value
I	9
T	12
D	3
A	10
	___
we get a total of the familiar	34

By adding the numerical values of the letters overlined on the reverse[97]

line	letter	numerical value
13)	B	13
13)	N	8
14)	K	6
15)	S	11
15)	A	10
15)	A	10
16)	A	10
		___
we get a total of		68

These enciphered totals, adding up to 34 and 68, show that we are dealing with a cryptographic text. The runemaster felt no obligation to conceal his riddles beneath a smooth plaintext (such as the scribes of the Paraiba, Vinland Map, and Kensington inscriptions achieved). Nevertheless, before going on, let us single out the words or phrases that by themselves suggest some meaning:

In line 2, "17 DID" means "17 dead." This need not record any historic fact. Both the Paraiba and Kensington texts use the expression "10 dead (or died)" as a cryptographic indicator.

In line 3, "AHR 1010" means "year 1010."

In line 4, "12 RISI UIST 12 NOR 10" is translatable as "12 (days?) journey west 12 north 10."

In line 5, "HAAKON FAN" signifies "Haakon found." "Haakon" is too common a name for us to pinpoint historically.

In line 6, "AT UIST" means "to west, westward."

In line 8, "AHR 1011" means "year 1011."

In line 10, "SIKLA SHIBI" is "sail(ed) ship(s)." The concept is appropriate enough for a marine expedition, but the use of SIKLA was specifically prompted because it stands for the date (6 October 1123), as we have shown above. The reader is tipped off by the anagrams of SIKLA; to wit, KILSA in line 1, and SILKA in line 7. SHIB recurs in line 13.

In lines 13-14, "UIDH AKI" could mean "with Aki," a known Old Norse name.

The name of the author or leader is to be expected in runic texts such as those from Spirit Pond. Alf Mongé has, with characteristic acumen, found the name of Henricus several times in these runestones. We shall reproduce only one of the examples. To do this we must transliterate the opening lines of the text with strict regard for the vertical alignment in the original:

1)   S Ī K A T̄ U M OD̄ I N:K I L S A : S(L+I)Ā:
2) 1 7: D I D : H A L A   D H I R:M I B A I N B Ā D
3) HUM: A   H R :   X X: ?? ULISA   SUITNK

The layout is significant. We are to reckon with line 1 until the first word-divider, at which point we drop immediately below on line 2 where we stop at the following divider. This gives us

SĪKAŢUMOĐIN:

HIR:

If we extract from these letters, the following: SKUINHIR, we have an anagram for HINRIKUS = "Henricus" (since I also covers E in the 16-rune alphabet, and in all runic systems K represents Latin C). The overlined letters are not part of the anagram, nor are A, M, and O which are not letters in the name "Henricus." They are instead explicable as his declaration of religious faith. If they stand for Latin *amo* "I love," perhaps the object of this verb remains to be detected in the text. But there is another possibility: Since AVM (in Latin!) is an abbreviation in the Kensington Stone for A(ve) V(irgo) M(aria) "Hail, Virgin Mary," maybe AMO is also a pious abbreviation such as A(ve) M(aria) O(ra [pro nobis]) "Hail Mary, pray (for us)."

Other items in the three lines are of cryptographic interest regarding the date. KILSA is an anagram of SIKLA "sailed" with an encipherment of the date, as we have already seen. The group that follows it, S(L+I)A, may convey the sense of "slew" for it is followed by "17 dead." But it has at the same time the numerical values of 11-23-10 = the year 1123, tenth month.

The layout may also have been calculated to detach LIS on line 3, for it can be marked off by dropping a vertical line below the divider after HIR in line 2, and another vertical line below the divider after KILSA in line 1. Mongé interprets LIS numerologically because the runes stand for 14+9+11 = 34 (the number which confirms the year 1123 as already explained).

We have reviewed enough of the Spirit Pond Runestones to show that in contrast to their plaintext gibberish, their cryptographic dimension is an almost endless labyrinth of ingenuity.

The runemasters obviously gave priority to their cryptograms without trying to provide a deceptively smooth cover text.

The controversy over the age and authenticity of the Spirit Pond Runestones, is based on the false premise that every rune-master had to compose only idiomatic plaintext, phrased gram-matically and spelled correctly. What the critics demand are Old Norse compositions that would be graded "A" if turned in today by a doctoral candidate in Scandinavian Studies. The philolo-gian who would understand the records of the past, must realize that ancient authors often had goals that differed drastically from our own. It would make a lot more *modern* sense if the runestones recorded in plaintext: "Henricus's expedition to Vin-land was celebrated on 6 October 1123." But many a medieval runemaster felt that such simple expression was for simpletons, not for the educated elite. If we attempt to formulate their atti-tude, we can do no better than recall Proverbs 1:6 which tells us that the cultivated person is one trained not only "to understand the words of the wise" but also "their riddles."

CHAPTER VII

Perspective and Conclusions

There are a number of false impressions that have gained wide currency. One of them is that no pre-Columbian inscription in any Old World script or language has ever been found in America. To lay this myth to rest, we point to an ancient text, professionally excavated in an unbroken archaeological context. The Bat Creek inscription is in the Hebrew language and Old Hebrew script of about A.D. 100. It was excavated in the late 1880s in Loudon County, eastern Tennessee, by the Smithsonian Institution, then published upside down in the official report dated 1894, and is now preserved in the Smithsonian Museum, Washington, D.C., together with the field notes and the whole archaeological assemblage of which it is a part.[98] There is no mystery, scandal, or skullduggery of any kind connected with the Bat Creek inscription. It proves human contact between the East Mediterranean and the southeastern U.S.A. in Roman times.

The Society for American Archaeology met at Santa Fe, New Mexico, in May 1968 to discuss pre-Columbian contacts between the Old World and the New. Riley-Kelley-Pennington-Rands 1971, p. 448, sum up the conference as follows: "It seems to be the consensus in the symposium and in the archaeological litera-

THE BAT CREEK INSCRIPTION

This Hebrew inscription of about A.D. 100 was excavated in an unrifled grave in Tennessee by the Smithsonian Institution. On the long line of writing, which runs from right to left, after the little word-divider the text reads: LYHWD [ ] "for Judea" or "for the Judea[ns]."

ture in general that there are, to date—excluding the Viking contacts discussed above [i.e. the excavation at L'Anse aux Meadows; but denying the authenticity of all the runic inscriptions found in America]—no verified archaeological finds of artifacts from one hemisphere in pre-Columbian context in the other." This statement represents the orthodox professional viewpoint and cannot be brushed aside with a mere denial.

Not all evidence is equally compelling. We shall call incontrovertible evidence "hard," and less convincing evidence "soft." Let us start with so-called soft evidence, limiting ourselves to examples that are of exceptional interest with a chance of leading to productive results and new directions.

The Bible tells us of a distant gold-bearing land called Ophir. King Solomon's fleets sailed there from the Red Sea port of Ezion-geber, near Elath, Israel, bringing back rich cargoes of gold. The question is: where was Ophir located? Dr. Robert Stieglitz, Curator of the National Maritime Museum in Haifa, Israel, calls my attention to a world map of biblical lands published in the sixteenth century; to wit, Arias Montanus 1571. That distinguished Spanish scholar indicates Ophir by the number "19" which he puts in two places: on the Andean coast of South America and the Rocky Mountain coast of North America. He thus implies that Solomon's fleets reached Ophir by crossing the Indian and Pacific oceans. As far as the Andes are concerned, Arias Montanus might have gotten the idea from the gold that Pizarro had already plundered from the Incan empire in Peru. But as far as I know, the Rocky Mountain gold was not known until much after the days of Arias Montanus (1527–1598). We are familiar with it from the Gold Rush of 1849. Since the 1571 map clearly indicates the Pacific coast of North (as well as South) America, Stieglitz notes that a tradition (perhaps cartographic) may have preserved, down to the sixteenth century A.D., memories of the mining of gold in the Rockies during the First Early Iron Age (1200–900 B.C.), for Solomon reigned in the tenth century B.C. Objections might take the form of supposing that Arias Montanus indicated Ophir "off the top of his head" without any factual evidence. Another criticism might be some presumed post-Columbian discovery and exploitation of gold in the Rockies prior to 1571, which was kept secret though somehow Arias Montanus got wind of it. Such criticisms are conceivable but not likely. If Steiglitz's insight proves to be correct, the historic implications of a trade route from the Near East across the Pacific to America in the Early Iron Age will be enormous.

Since Near East archaeologists date Syro-Hittite art at roughly the same time as Americanists date the "danzantes" of Monte Alban (very approximately, 800 B.C.), it is natural to regard resemblances as perhaps reflecting historical contact. Not only do the bearded figurines in Monte Alban suggest Old World races, but the carved slabs in both areas are used as orthostats to provide interior mural decoration.

Now for another illustration of so-called soft evidence: A deified ruler, identified by the Zapotec sign for the numeral "1," seems to be (as noted by Joan K. Gordon) the Creator or

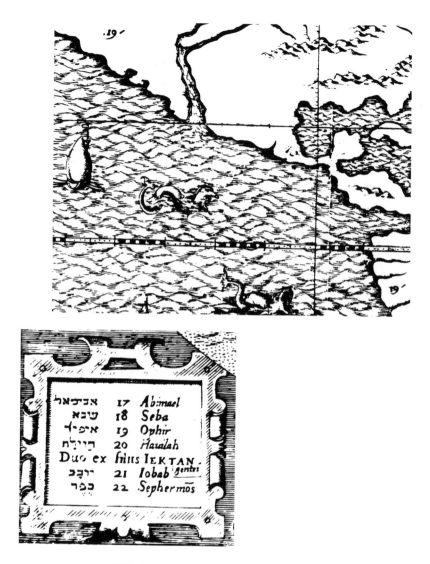

THE MAP OF BIBLICAL GEOGRAPHY

This map "for facilitating the explanation of Holy Scriptures" was prepared by Benedictus Arias Montanus (1527–1598) and published in Antwerp in 1571. The map is a copper engraving, 32 x 53 cm. It indicates the gold-bearing land of biblical Ophir by the number "19" on the west coast of both North and South America. By 1571 Arias Montanus would have heard of the gold pillaged by Pizarro from the Incan Empire, but hardly of the North American sources of gold now famous since the Gold Rush of 1849. If Arias Montanus is indeed reflecting an esoteric tradition about the ancient exploitation of gold in the Rocky Mountains, archaeologists should eventually find the old gold-mining installations there. We now have at our disposal still more methods of procedure and testing than those successfully used for dating the working of ancient copper mines in the Wadi Araba (between the Dead Sea and the Gulf of Aqaba) in 1934, and more recently on Crete. (Photo by courtesy of Robert Stieglitz)

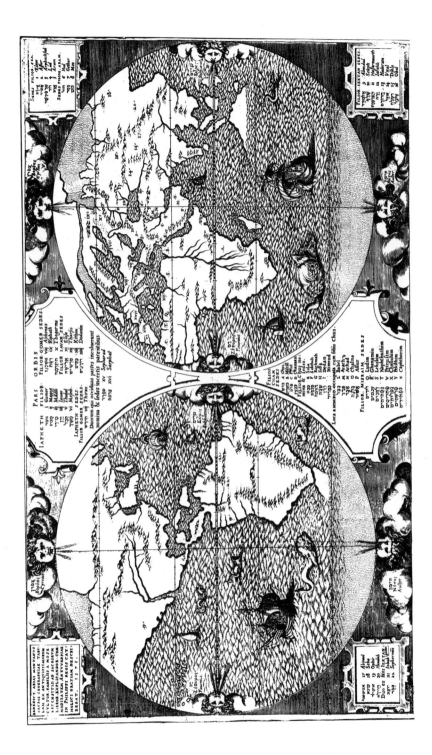

DEIFIED ZAPOTEC RULER

This stucco head of about A.D. 700 is above the tomb of a Zapotec ruler at Lambityeco, Oaxaca, Mexico. The Zapotec glyph for the numeral "1" (above the head) attributes to the ruler the role of the "One" associated with the divine Creator in Mesoamerica as well as in the Ancient Near East. The phenomenon of deified kings is widespread. (Courtesy of Foto A. v. Wuthenau)

head of the pantheon (for a photograph see Wuthenau 1972, front cover). Mesoamerica and the ancient Near East confront us with the phenomenon of deified numbers. "One" is the designation of the Creator in both areas (Gordon 1971, p. 150 and note 138 on p. 205). But numerology haunts many people, so why must we assume that similar systems in Mesoamerica and the Old World are historically related? In any such system it would not be unnatural to assign the first number to the great god. The

THE PHYLACTERY STELA

This stone stela from Tepatlaxco, Veracruz, Mexico, is in the National Museum, Mexico City. Some scholars date it around A.D. 100 while others attribute it to the Early Classical period ca. A.D. 300. In any case it is about contemporary with the age of maximum Roman expansion.

The main bearded figure holds his right arm half-raised. A strip (of leather?) is wound spirally around the forearm and palm, and then fastened around the thumb and the other fingers. The bent head of the attendant hides whatever was worn above the elbow (e.g., a phylactery box). The object held by a strip on the forehead may possibly be the phylactery box worn on the head.

There are variant phylactery traditions practiced by different groups of Jews today. The hand-phylactery is now worn on the weaker arm; i.e., on the left arm of right-handed men, and on the right arm of left-handed men. This stela shows it on the right arm. The finger-windings still vary according to several traditional schools. (Courtesy of Foto A.v. Wuthenau)

beard of the Zapotec god suggests contacts with the white race, but bearded Indians have failed to impress die-hard independent inventionists. In any discussion that is to prove fruitful, we cannot limit ourselves to repeating the same old facts.

Joan K. Gordon has also made the sharp observation that the Tepatlaxco Stela depicts a hero wearing phylacteries such as those worn ceremonially by observant Jewish males while reciting their daily morning prayers.[99] The personage has wrapped the phylactery strip around his arm seven times as Jews still do. Since there are variant Jewish traditions in such matters, it is no counterindication that the finger windings differ from standard Jewish usages today. The fact is that different Jewish groups practice different finger-windings. It would be simplistic to attribute the Mexican Stela necessarily to a Jewish migration, for there is every reason to believe that the wearing of such phylacteries was widespread, and not limited to Jews in antiquity.

Mrs. Roberta Richards has noted that on the Phaistos Disc (from Crete, ca. 1500 B.C.), the hand sign depicts a strip wrapped around the wrist (coming down from the forearm) and thumb.[100] Such wrappings cannot serve purely utilitarian ends. They have a ritual function. The phenomenon can be traced back to the Uruk Age (before 3000 B.C.) in Mesopotamia, for, as Miss Martha Morrison calls to my attention, the earliest form of the Sumerian sign $\acute{A} = idu$ "hand" has wrappings (this time not in a single spiral but criss-crossed) the length of the arm and on the thumb.[101]

Another example of so-called soft evidence: Wuthenau (1972) has pointed out that on a Stela from Campeche, Mexico, a man wearing a reed-boat hat, has an earplug with the Star of David. The Star of David first appears in Palestine at Megiddo in a Solomonic context. Americanists regard the sign as the year glyph. (The Star of David definitely appears on the Stone of Uxmal; see Wuthenau 1972, p. 11 and back cover.) Whichever way we choose to interpret the Star (and who is to say that men cannot invent the six-pointed star independently by combining two triangles?), the fact is that a boat-hat suggests some important navigator. Again it was Joan K. Gordon who observed that the Campeche navigator has birds in front of him, calling to mind the birds associated with the biblical Noah and the Babylonian Utnapishtim in the Gilgamesh Epic. Those flood heroes sent birds from the ark to find out if there was any dry land.

THE CAMPECHE FLOOD HERO
The role of the man on this Late Classic Mayan stone stela from Campeche is suggested by his boat-shaped hat. This is confirmed by some of the other details, such as the two birds; one on his chest, the other just left of the two upper squares that he faces. Birds are used by the Flood Hero in the Mesopotamian Gilgamesh Epic as well as in Genesis. This stela is in the National Museum, Mexico City. (Courtesy of Foto A.v. Wuthenau)

There is no use in pointing out such parallels if our aim is to establish contacts between the Old and New Worlds that *all* rational people will have to accept, *regardless of their viewpoints.* And this brings us to the subject of this book: the hard evidence of inscriptions. No one who knows about the Bat Creek Stone can subscribe to the negative summation of the Sante Fe symposium. Triangles and even Stars of David may be independently invented, but not the Hebrew (or any other) language and script. An ancient Hebrew inscription found *in situ* with a whole archaeological assemblage in Tennessee by the Smithsonian can only mean pre-Columbian contact across the Atlantic. The contact took place by ship, and illustrates why we must be aware of ancient man's seacraft and navigational capabilities, if we are to understand history.

The problem of Old World inscriptions found accidentally in America has forced us to devise a method for determining authenticity. If such an inscription anticipates *future* discoveries in sufficient detail to rule out accidental luck on the part of a forger, it must be genuine.

I applied this method to the plaintext of the Paraiba Inscription, but some critics didn't like it. Mongé applied the method to the cryptograms of American runestones, but again some of the critics didn't like it. The Vinland Map Conference had the general effect of undermining confidence among scholars, because of the *non sequitur* that skepticism and science are synonymous. Blind denial is no more valid than blind acceptance.

This book has taken each of the component problems out of its isolation and put them into historical perspective with one another. Mesopotamian acrostics go back to the second millennium, but the acrostic-telestic expressing the name and religious devotion of the author has been traced back to a scientifically excavated tablet of the eighth century B.C. When we find Bishop Henricus using a sophisticated acrostic-telestic (whose existence none of the participants of the Vinland Map Conference even suspected) to express his name and religious devotion, we are dealing with a genuine historic development; not with a modern forgery by a rogue or prankster who writes Latin in authentic medieval script, with ink from an old recipe, on his private stock of ancient parchment, and with a stable of worms trained to enhance the illusion of his wares' authenticity.

The Paraiba, Kensington, and Spirit Pond texts have cryptograms confirming dates by their double. This feature locks the three texts in together as examples of the same historic development.

The acrostic-telestic anagrams, with both halves unscrambled by the same key, join the Paraiba and Vinland Map texts as illustrations of one and the same historic development. Here too there is a carry-over of message content, for both include a formulation of religious faith.

To assail the authenticity of the foregoing inscriptions, it has become necessary to demonstrate a plot stretching at least from 1872 to 1971. A ring of forgers or pranksters must be shown to have operated in Brazil, Minnesota, Maine, and Europe. They must also have somehow forged and planted the eighth century B.C. Khorsabad tablet excavated by the University of Chicago in 1932.

The hypothetical ring of forgers had amazingly wide intellectual resources. They knew how to compose Babylonian, Canaanite. Latin, and Norse texts, and write them in their proper ancient scripts. They possessed and transmitted intricate cryptograms that the leading experts of cryptography have known nothing about for centuries. Moreover, inspired by the Devil, they anticipated the future discovery of linguistic elements.

Clever forgers keep up to date. It would not be surprising if they soon produce inscriptions with cryptograms such as those described in this book. Then we shall have to wait and see whether or not *subsequently* excavated texts bear out their authenticity. But the documents we have analyzed and evaluated will stand as evidence of contacts across the Atlantic in the sixth century B.C. (at the latest), again in Roman times, and finally in the twelfth and fourteenth centuries A.D.

We are intentionally omitting any estimate of the effect these contacts had on pre-Columbian civilization in America. This book aims instead at fixing the cornerstones of hard evidence that provide specific contacts by definite people at definite times. We are not interested in pushing any special interests: Semitic, Roman, Nordic, etc. If a real world history is someday to be written, we must first establish the actual contacts in time and place.

There is no need to join either of the warring camps in the chronic and ill-tempered battle between the diffusionists and in-dependent inventionists. Any school of thought that commits us to conclusions regardless of the facts cannot serve the cause of truth. Let us make no mistake about it: all schools of thought are in reality "schools of un-thought" to the extent that they prevent us from going where the facts should lead us.

The greatest obstacle we face is the general confusion between consensus of opinion and objective truth. The media are oper-ated by people, often well-meaning, who cannot be experts on all of the wide spectrum of subjects they write up. Their normal pro-cedure is first to get the story from the person who claims to have achieved something newsworthy. In the case of innovations, they then usually check up by making phone calls to other "experts." The latter are generally taken unawares at their desks while working on entirely different matters. If a friend's work is being written up, they have to say something nice. If it is a rival's work, they may denigrate or contradict, but often insist that their names not be mentioned. Yet let us suppose that there is no per-sonal prejudice. The very fact that it is an innovation means that it is not in keeping with the consensus of opinion. Politically as-tute people never buck consensus. Crusaders for the truth will buck it (and afterwards pay the price). The question that matters is not "Does the majority like it?" but "Does the innovation fol-low from the primary facts?"

The intelligent reader will judge for himself. Those who apply the test of opinion research are in a different category. Without examining the facts fully and fairly, there is no way of knowing whether *vox populi* is really *vox dei* or merely *vox asinorum*.

NOTES

1. Wilson 1969 (see Bibliography).

2. The polemic is accurately described by Castro 1971.

3. Gordon 1968a and b.

4. See Holand 1962, pp. 161–76.

5. For the negative approach, see Blegen 1968 and Wahlgren 1958.

6. Holand 1962, pp. 313–41.

7. E.g., Kvamme 1967.

8. Mongé-Landsverk 1967, and Landsverk 1969.

9. Kahn 1967.

10. Haugen 1972 opts for forgery. Noteworthy is the statement on page 77: "The one solid fact that emerges from this examination of the inscriptions is that they cannot be explained without taking into account the Kensington Stone inscription in Minnesota. One's conclusions from this fact will depend on how one views that stone." By rejecting the testimony of the cryptograms, he manages to adhere to the conclusions he published thirty years earlier (Haugen 1942). As we shall see in Chapter V, the Kensington Stela is genuine.

11. The earliest major language to be recorded is Sumerian; Egyptian followed soon after. See Gordon 1968c.

12. Namely, Professor Harry Torczyner (now Tur-Sinai) of Hebrew University.

13. Pritchard 1955, p. 93, n. 190.

14. Sēfer Yᵉṣîrāh 1961–62 and Stenring 1970.

15. As plaintext, ŠŠK is meaningless gibberish. The reader should remember this when dealing with the criticism that a genuine ancient or medieval inscription cannot contain gibberish. To the contrary it is gibberish that often alerts us to the presence of a cryptogram.

16. As plaintext, LB QMY might mean "the heart of those who rise against me" but no one speaking or writing straightforward Hebrew would use such an awkward expression. "Bad" Hebrew, Latin, or Old Norse is often, in the inscriptions discussed in this book, an indication of a cryptogram.

17. The contexts (Jeremiah 25 and 51) tell us that "Babylon" (25:1, 11, 12, etc.; 51:1, 41, 42, etc.) and its people the "Chaldeans" are meant.

18. See Leviticus 4:12 for ŠPK in the sense of "rubbish heap, dump."

19. Gordon 1967, text 142.

20. This acrostic occurs in the Sibylline Oracles (8:217–43). It is conveniently quoted in Marcus 1947, p. 113, though with one error (XREISTOS has been modified by Marcus to the common form XRISTOS).

21. E.g., Craig 1895, text K 7592, plates 29–31. The scribe divides the text into sections of two or three lines each. The first sign of the opening line of each section starts at the far left. All other lines are indented. The first section begins with the sign for *a*, the next section with *na*, the third section with *ku*. Reading down, *a-na-ku* is the pronoun "I."

22. Marcus 1947, p. 109.

23. The text was published by Lambert 1968, pp. 130–32.

24. Sweet 1969 first recognized that there is a telestic as well as an acrostic. He calls the acrostic-telestic a "double acrostic."

25. The sign at the end of line 9 is polyphonous. Among its values are *tú* and *liḫ*. *Tú* is to be pronounced when the line is read horizontally, but *liḫ* when the telestic is read down vertically.

26. There is a literature of varying quality on Columbus's secret signature:

.S.
.S.A.S.
X M Y

See Madariaga 1940, pages 403–4, 503 for a preliminary discussion and references to earlier studies. Columbus wanted his heirs to perpetuate this secret signature. While the last word has not yet been written on interpreting it, a case has been made for Jewish elements of a kabbalistic nature. Columbus elsewhere does not use dots in his signatures. The triangle of Ss flanked by dots smacks of kabbalism, calling to mind *Sanctus Sanctus Sanctus:* the translation of *qādôs qādôš qādôš* "Holy Holy Holy" in Isaiah 6:3. The whole verse is *qādôš qādôš qādôš ʾᵃdônāy ṣᵉbāʾôt mᵉlôʾ kol-hâʾāres kᵉbôdō* "Holy, Holy, Holy is Adonay Sebaoth [Lord of Hosts], all the earth is full of His glory." The A may stand for "Adonay" and an S may be doing double duty for "Sebaoth." A factor in the argument is the use of S and A in Sephardic prayer books with Spanish translations. The subject should be reopened in the new light of the deep and ancient roots of secret signatures with declarations of religious faith. Madariaga has delineated perceptively the crypto-Jewish background and connections of Columbus. To follow Madariaga it is necessary to understand the phenomenon of conversion under pressure in Spain. Such conversion by Columbus's ancestors did not as a rule carry any resolution or desire to revert to Judaism, though it could preserve a mystical devotion to the religion of one's forefathers. The magnitude of the Jewish impact on Christian Spain is portrayed by Castro 1954, pp. 466–588.

27. Kahn 1967, p. 82.

28. Arntz 1944, pp. 268–69, 274, plate 5 (figure 16); and Krause 1943, page 44, plate 12 (figure 23).

29. In the light of this authentic text (and there are others), I cannot understand Haugen (1972, p. 74) who declares the Spirit Pond texts as modern forgeries because: "Either the text would be wholly gibberish so that one could look for a scrambled alphabet, or else it would make sense as it stands." Runestones of unquestioned authenticity make it quite clear that some are entirely meaningful as plaintext, some are entirely gibberish as plaintext, while others are mixed. The gibberish, to be sure, is often the vehicle for hidden meaning. See further Landsverk 1973b.

30. Sweet 1969.

31. Gordon 1971, pages 120–27.

32. Gordon 1968a, page 79; Gordon 1968b, page 433.

33. Van den Branden 1968, page 57.

34. Harden 1962, p. 120, figure 35.

35. Donner-Röllig 1962–64, vol. III, plate III, text 73 (mistakenly labeled "79").

36. Van den Branden 1968, page 57, feels that only five letters (K, L, S, Q, and T) suggest the late sixth century B.C., while all the rest could appear in texts of the ninth or even tenth century B.C. (We should remember, however, that in such matters, it is the latest, not the earliest, elements that point to the date.)

37. Herodotus 1946–1957, vol. II, pages 238–41.

38. We shall see in Chapter VI that Bjarni Herjulfson's sighting of North America was accidental, but the rest of the known Norse voyages to North America (touched off by Bjarni's reports) were intentional.

39. Donner-Röllig 1962–64 has examples: e.g., texts 26, 181, etc., for listing sacrifices; and 14, 32, 33, 39, 40, etc., for dates.

40. Gordon 1968a, page 76.

41. Delekat 1969, pages 7, 19–20.

42. Judges 15:16.

43. Judges 5:30. For the omission of the -m in ḤBLTY', note YDY (yāday) in Ezekiel 13:18 instead of normal "absolute" YDYM "2 hands" (Fontinoy 1969, p. 58. See also the absolute duals without -m/n listed by Fontinoy on pages 93, 107, 108, 112, 124, 125, 126).

44. This in turn was not sensed by runologists or even by the cryptanalysts until the Paraiba Stone was brought to bear on the problem.

45. Gordon 1968b, pages 428–29.

46. Gordon 1968a, page 79, Gordon 1968b, page 429.

47. While "one" for "a" does not become common until later (and it is very common in later Aramaic dialects), there are examples in the general period of the Paraiba text. Thus Esther 3:8 (ᶜam-'eḥād "a people"). While this usage is not frequent in Old Testament times, it is, however, attested in Hebrew well before the sixth century B.C. (1 Samuel 6:7; 24:15; 26:20; 1 Kings 19:4, 5). In the Paraiba text there are no elements that first came into existence after the sixth century B.C.

48. Delekat 1969, page 7.

49. Marcus 1947 covers this topic well.

50. The choice of spelling *kī*, K or KY, already existed in the Late Bronze Age when the Ugaritic tablets were written. In Ugaritic, *kī* is normally written K, but occasionally also KY (Gordon 1967, page 416, no. 1183).

51. Exodus 6:20; Numbers 26:59.

52. Gordon 1966, page 24.

53. First observed by Joan K. Gordon.

54. Regularly mistranslated "became Jews" (i.e., converted to Judaism). In a "millet" society (= one made up of ethnoreligious minorities) survival through dissimulation, not conversion, is what each group practices in time of fear. The Hebrew conjugation known as the *hitpa^{c}el* (as in *hityah^{e}dū* "they pretended to be Jewish") frequently has the function of pretending.

55. 1 Kings 9:26–28.

56. Herodotus 7:89. See Gordon 1972, page 15.

57. The notion that vowel letters are anachronistic in a sixth century B.C. inscription, is belied by their presence in the sixth century B.C. ostraca excavated at Lachish (Gordon 1968b, page 432).

58. The reader should refer back to the text (preferably to the transcription above, with the acrostic-telestic letters underlined) to follow the argument.

59. Even the strangest of the words can be explained as correct without emendation. For example ^{c}ṢWN in line 4 (in the place name Ezion-geber) would be more familiar as either ^{c}ṢYWN or ^{c}ṢYN with Y. In 1874 Schlottmann was able to explain ^{c}ṢWN through biblical evidence (Gordon 1968a, p. 79) and we can now add a new approach from Ugaritic. Hebrew *Ṣîdôn(îm)* "Sidon(ians)" corresponds to ṢDYN(M) in Ugaritic. The Paraiba form ^{c}ṢWN is thus related to normal Hebrew ^{c}ṢYWN as Hebrew *Ṣîdôn(îm)* "Sidon(ians)" is to Ugaritic ṢDYN(M).

60. This is the way *socij* (describing the relationship between Bjarni and Leif) is generally interpreted. But if *socij* (line 3) is translated "partners" (as distinct from "traveling companions"), a case can be made for their partnership inasmuch as it was on Bjarni's former ship that Leif sailed.

61. See Herbert C. Taylor, "Vinland and the Way Thither" in Riley-Kelley-Pennington-Rands 1971, pages 242–54.

62. For a full discussion of the viewpoints, see Washburn 1971. Some of them are spelled out at the end of this chapter.

63. Mongé-Landsverk 1967, page 145, and Landsverk 1973a.

64. The omission of *n* at the end of a syllable is familiar to Latinists, and occurs in this text: note *omnipotētis* for *omnipotentis* in line 7, and *volūtati* for *voluntati* in lines 8-9.

65. Allegro 1965, pp. 54–56.

66. Which, however, Haugen 1972 considers faked because he refuses to countenance the existence of the cryptograms.

67. I.e., for this inscription and others (such as Spirit Pond Runestone #3) in which the *th-* sign also covers *d*.

68. A practical cause of this curiosity was the dearth of productive land at the disposal of the Norsemen. They had colonized various islands in the North Atlantic and Arctic oceans, including the Hebrides, Orkneys, Shetlands, Faeroes, Iceland, and Greenland. But survival in all those areas was hard, especially in Greenland. They needed a less severe climate and a more fertile soil. In spite of their seamanship and trade, their life-style (unlike that of the Eskimos) required animal husbandry, dairy farming, and some agriculture. Other considerations, like the spread of Christianity to the Skraelings (as they called the Eskimos and Indians), were secondary.

69. Much of the controversy over the Kensington Stela has been occasioned by the unrecognized restrictions imposed on the runemaster by the cryptograms. To meet the requirements of their cryptograms, the runemasters often indulge in strange constructions and misspellings. As long as there was no awareness of the cryptograms (and such was the case until the late 1960s), the philologians found the plaintext belabored, inconsistent, and "therefore spurious." Once this reaction became established as the one and only "scientific" possibility, many minds remained closed to new evidence. The best statement of the established evaluation (long before the discovery of the cryptograms) is Haugen 1942, pages 156–57.

70. Elliott 1959, page 1, points out that the German verb "raunen" still preserves the flavor of secrets and mystery. Elliott's judicious conclusion is worth keeping in mind: "The view that runes and magic were intimately linked has not gone unchallenged, but there are weightier arguments in its favor than against it" (page 2).

71. Holand 1962, pp. 313–41, and Kvamme 1967. Morison 1971, pages 75–79, is a typical illustration of negation and jeering based on smug ignorance.

72. Columbus sailed in 1477 to "Tile" = Thule = Iceland. While this voyage is generally admitted, a number of writers insist that Columbus learned nothing in Iceland. Although Columbus does not specifically state that he heard stories about Vinland, it is hard to justify dogmatic denials that he heard anything significant in Iceland. In any case, knowledge of the Norse voyages to America had become part of Latin learning from the eleventh century to the Age of Columbus (e.g., Erik Wahlgren, in Washburn 1971, p. 135).

73. Gordon 1971, page 42.

74. See Mongé-Landsverk 1967, pages 77–97 for the various cryptograms including the one providing the exact date.

75. Ingstad 1969.

76. Anderson 1906.

77. Haugen 1942 provides the most critical and factual account.

78. Holand 1962 has the merit of being an indefatigable pioneer but his work is tinged with the weaknesses resulting from his early detachment from academic life.

79. Pohl 1972. There are contradictions between the two sagas (and vis-à-vis several minor sources). Our account is a blending and abridgement with no pretense of being a factual history in every detail. We are after all dealing with saga, not chronicles. For the problems, see Haugen 1942, pages 97–169. Our account does not incorporate all the sagas. We have for example omitted the tales about Bjarni Grimolfson and the horrors of Freydis which Wahlgren (in Washburn 1971, p. 134) is inclined to regard as unhistorical.

80. Holand 1962, page 16. The fact that this tale is not discussed by most of the authorities on the subject, suggests that its historicity should not be assumed without investigation.

81. For the sites and remains of the Norse colonists on Greenland, see Ingstad 1966.

82. This may mean little more than that Vinland was sufficiently south of Greenland to have perceptibly longer days in midwinter. In the Icelandic text, *eyktar stad* is mentioned first, reflecting a usage whereby the 24-hour day begins at sunset: the system incidentally that the Hebrews have used, from biblical times (note "and there was evening and morning: day one" in Genesis 1:5) down to current Jewish religious usage.

83. In Scandinavian *vin* means "vine" as well as "wine," so that "Vinland" conveys the sense of both "Wine Land" and "Vine Land."

84. This is a typical detail in a Nordic text dealing with travel. It is paralleled in the Kensington Stela. The Norsemen knew how to live off the seas on which they sailed.

85. The small number of women among so many men is characteristic of Old Norse voyages. Note also that the Paraiba text mentions three women among twelve men.

86. Erik Wahlgren is right in insisting that while L'Anse aux Meadows is the site of a Norse colony, Vinland lay farther south (Washburn 1971, p. 134). SP-1 indicates that HOOP (= Spirit Pond, Maine) is in Vinland.

87. The Norse of Greenland were so inbred that Pope Alexander III ca. 1160 instructed the Archbishop of Nidros (also spelled "Nidaros" = modern Trondheim) to grant a dispensation to islanders dwelling twelve or more days from Norway (= apparently the Greenlanders), to marry their kin legitimately because it was difficult, and for the poor impossible, to find wives elsewhere (Oystein Ore, in Washburn 1971, p. 146).

88. "City" here does not mean a great population center, but rather the site of a cathedral or bishop's seat.

89. Unless otherwise documented, the papal letters quoted are assembled in Anderson 1906, pp. 131–76.

90. These are low estimates. The total Norse population of Greenland probably did not exceed three thousand in any case.

91. Mongé-Landsverk 1967, pp. 98–102.

92. The Norse presence in Greenland is attested epigraphically in the fourteenth century by the Narssaq inscription containing the enciphered date of Advent Sunday, 28 November 1316. The artistically beautiful, inscribed runic horn from Winnetka, Illinois, is dated in 1329. The authenticity of the Narssaq text is not challenged be-

cause it was found in Greenland. This is of course not the case with the Winnetka Horn found in the United States. From the photographs and cryptanalysis of the Horn sent to me by Mongé, I have every reason to consider it genuine. Mongé's solutions of the Narssaq and Winnetka inscriptions are in Landsverk in 1973a.

It has been suggested that Paul Knutson's mission carried him to continental America and provides the specific historical background for the Kensington Stela of 1362. Without documentary proof, this must remain a mere theory.

93. SP-3 obviously confronts us with anagrams of this word; SIKLA occurs in line 10, but KILSA in line 1 and SILKA in line 7.

94. The fact that they are eight in number (possibly keyed in with the eight runes of MILTIAKI) may turn out to be a cryptogram for the eight-letter name of Henricus.

95. The reason ✝ , with the horizontal line, must be used, is that without that line, a hypothetical bindrune ↾ (for ↾ + |) would be indistinguishable from plain ↾ L.

96. The monograms are intentional for, like the bindrunes, they count as only one letter in the cryptograms. For example, an anagram of SIKLA is enciphered in the first five lines which lack pentathic numbers. The key is the number of words on the line, indicating that we are to select the letter which is that far from the beginning of the line:

Line	No. of words	Opening letters
1)	3	SIK̲
5)	4	UN̲K : S̲
6)	4	HR(I+N)I̲
7)	3	SIL̲
9)	2	BA̲

The letters thus indicated are KSILA, an anagram of SILKA. Note that in line 6 the monogram I+N must be treated as a single letter for the sake of the cryptogram. Mongé has demonstrated still other examples in a complex cryptogram yielding not only KSILA but also the anagrammed name of "Henricus" and the number "68" (published fully in Landsverk 1973a).

97. The overlined letters after line 1 on the obverse are also significant cryptographically. What makes their solution difficult is that there are several letters above which it is hard to tell whether the scribe has incised a line or whether the surface has been accidentally scratched.

98. See Gordon 1972 for a detailed study of the script and interpretation of the text, as well as the discussion of other discoveries (including the professionally excavated Roman head from Calixtlauaca) that demonstrate contacts between the Mediterranean and America around the second century A.D.

99. A photograph has been published in the *National Geographic*, Oct. 1968, on p. 504 (upper left). The date (ca. A.D. 100) is about the same as that of the Bat Creek Stone and the Roman head from Calixtlauaca.

100. See Gordon 1971, pp. 97–98 for the photographs.

101. Labat 1963, pp. 152–53.

BIBLIOGRAPHY

Allegro 1965:

John Marco Allegro, *The Shapira Affair,* Doubleday, Garden City, N.Y.

Anderson 1906:

Rasmus B. Anderson (who signs the introduction, though no author's name is on the title page), *The Flatey Book and Recently Discovered Vatican Manuscripts Concerning America as Early as the Tenth Century,* Norroena Society, London, Stockholm, Copenhagen, Berlin, New York.

Arias Montanus 1571:

Benedictus Arias Montanus, *Sacrae Geographiae Tabulam...,* Officina Plantina, Antwerp.

Arntz 1944:

Helmut Arntz, *Handbuch der Runenkunde,* 2nd ed., Max Niemeyer Verlag, Halle/Saale.

Blegen 1968:

Theodore C. Blegen, *The Kensington Rune Stone: New Light on an Old Riddle,* Minnesota Historical Society, St. Paul.

Budge, 1970:

E. A. Wallis Budge, *Amulets and Talismans.* Collier Books edition, Macmillan, New York.

Burgon 1972:

Glad Lynn Burgon, *An Analysis of Purported Ancient American Linear Inscriptions,* a doctoral dissertation of Brigham Young University, Provo, Utah.

Castro 1954:

Américo Castro, *The Structure of Spanish History,* Princeton University Press, Princeton.

Castro 1971:

Federico Perez Castro, "La 'Inscription' Fenicio-Cananea de Paraiba (Brasil)," *Anuario de Estudios Atlanticos,* No. 17, 1971, Patronato de la "Casa de Colon," Madrid–Las Palmas, pp. 307–33.

Craig 1895:

James A. Craig, *Assyrian and Babylonian Religious Texts* I, J.C. Hinrichs'sche Buchhandlung, Leipzig.

Delekat 1969:

Lienhard Delekat, *Phönizier in Amerika,* Peter Hanstein Verlag GMBH, Bonn.

Donner-Röllig 1962–64:

H. Donner and W. Röllig, *Kanaanäische und Aramäische Inschriften,* 3 volumes, Otto Harrassowitz, Wiesbaden.

Elliott 1959:

Ralph W. V. Elliott, *Runes: An Introduction*, Manchester University Press, Manchester.

Enterline 1972:

James Robert Enterline, *Viking America*, Doubleday, Garden City, N.Y.

Fontinoy 1969:

Charles Fontinoy, *Le duel dans les langues sémitiques*, Société d'Édition "Les Belles Lettres," Paris.

Garmonsway 1928:

G. N. Garmonsway, *An Early Norse Reader*, Cambridge University Press, Cambridge.

Gathorne-Hardy 1970:

G. M. Gathorne-Hardy, *The Norse Discoverers of America*, Clarendon Press, Oxford.

Gordon 1957:

E. V. Gordon, *An Introduction to Old Norse*, 2nd ed., revised by A.R. Taylor, Clarendon Press, Oxford.

Gordon 1966:

Cyrus H. Gordon, *Ugarit and Minoan Crete*, W.W. Norton, New York.

Gordon 1967:

Cyrus H. Gordon, *Ugaritic Textbook*, Pontifical Biblical Institute, Rome.

Gordon 1968a:

Cyrus H. Gordon, "The Authenticity of the Phoenician Text from Parahyba," *Orientalia* 37, pp. 75–80.

Gordon 1968b:

Cyrus H. Gordon, "The Canaanite Text from Brazil," *Orientalia* 37, pp. 425–36, 461–63.

Gordon 1968c:

Cyrus H. Gordon, *Forgotten Scripts*, Basic Books, New York.

Gordon 1971:

Cyrus H. Gordon, *Before Columbus*, Crown Publishers, New York.

Gordon 1972:

Cyrus H. Gordon, *Book of the Descendants of Doctor Benjamin Lee and Dorothy Gordon*, Ventnor Publishers, Ventnor, N.J.; Chapter I: "The Bat Creek Inscription."

Harden 1962:

Donald Harden, *The Phoenicians*, Praeger, New York.

Haugen 1942:

Einar Haugen, *Voyage to Vinland: The First American Saga*, newly translated and interpreted, Knopf, New York.

Haugen 1972:

Einar Haugen, *The Rune Stones of Spirit Pond, Maine,* reprinted from *Man in the Northeast,* No. 4, Box 148, Fitzwilliam, N.H.

Herodotus 1946–1957:

Herodotus with an English translation by A.D. Godley in four volumes, The Loeb Classical Library, Harvard University Press, Cambridge, Mass.; and Wm. Heinemann Ltd., London..

Holand 1962:

Hjalmar R. Holand, *Explorations in America before Columbus,* 2nd ed., 3rd printing, Twayne Publishers, Inc., New York.

Ingstad 1966:

Helge Marcus Ingstad, *Land under the Pole Star: A Voyage to the Norse Settlements of Greenland and the Saga of the People That Vanished,* translated from the Norwegian by Naomi Walford, St. Martin's Press, New York.

Ingstad 1969:

Helge Marcus Ingstad, *Westward to Vinland: The Discovery of Pre-Columbian Norse House-Sites in North America,* translated from the Norwegian by Erik J. Friis, St. Martin's Press, New York.

Junior 1970:

José Anthero Pereira Junior, "Em Tôrno da Velha Questão que é a de Terem Estado os Fenícios no Brasil e Outros Reparos," *Revista do Instituto Histórico e Geográfico de S. Paulo,* Vol. 68, pp. 183–90.

Kahn 1967:

David Kahn, *The Code Breakers: The Story of Secret Writing,* Macmillan, New York.

Krause 1943:

Wolfgang Krause, *Was Man in Runen Ritzte,* 2nd ed., Max Miemeyer Verlag, Halle/Saale.

Kvamme 1967:

Torvald Kvamme's communication dated 9 January 1967 in Johannes Kristoffer Tornöe, *Columbus in the Arctic?,* Oslo pp. 125-30.

Labat 1963:

René Labat, *Manuel d'Epigraphie Akkadienne,* 4th ed., Imprimerie Nationale, Paris.

Lambert 1968:

W.G. Lambert, "Literary Style in First Millennium Mesopotamia," *Journal of the American Oriental Society,* Volume 88, pp. 123–32.

Landsverk 1969:

O.G. Landsverk, *Ancient Norse Messages on American Stones,* Norseman Press, Glendale, California.

Landsverk 1973a:

O.G. Landsverk, *Runic Records of the Norsemen in America,* distributed by Twayne Publishers, New York.

Landsverk 1973b:

O. G. Landsverk, *The Spirit Pond Cryptography*, manuscript to be published as a fascicle of *Man in the Northeast*, Box 148, Fitzwilliam, N.H.

Madariaga 1940:

Salvador de Madariaga, *Christopher Columbus: Being the Life of the Very Magnificent Lord Don Cristóbal Colón*, Macmillan, New York.

Marcus 1947:

Ralph Marcus, "Alphabetic Acrostics in the Hellenistic and Roman Periods," *Journal of Near Eastern Studies*, Volume 6, pp. 109–15.

Mongé-Landsverk 1967:

Alf Mongé and O. G. Landsverk, *Norse Medieval Cryptography in Runic Carvings*, Norseman Press, Glendale, California.

Morison 1971:

Samuel Eliot Morison, *The European Discovery of America: The Northern Voyages* A.D. *500–1600*, Oxford University Press, New York.

Mowat 1965:

Farley Mowat, *Westviking: The Ancient Norse in Greenland and North America*, Little Brown, Boston.

Netto 1885:

Ladislau Netto, *Lettre à Monsieur Renan à propos de l'inscription Phénicienne apocryphe soumise en 1872 à l'Institut historique, géographique et ethnographique du Brésil*, Lombaerta & Comp., Rio de Janeiro.

Noreen 1970:

Adolf Noreen, *Altnordische Grammatik* I, University of Alabama Press, University, Alabama.

Pohl 1972:

Frederick J. Pohl, *The Viking Settlements of North America*, C.N. Potter, New York.

Pritchard 1955:

James B. Pritchard (ed.), *Ancient Near Eastern Texts*, 2nd ed., Princeton University Press, Princeton.

Riley-Kelley-Pennington-Rands 1971:

Carroll L. Riley, J. Charles Kelley, Campbell W. Pennington, Robert L. Rands (editors), *Man across the Seas: Problems of Pre-Columbian Contacts*, University of Texas, Austin, Texas.

Schalit 1973:

Abraham Schalit (ed.), *The World History of the Jewish People*, First Series, Volume 6 *(The Hellenistic Age)*, Rutgers University, New Brunswick, N.J.

Sēfer Yᵉṣîrāh 1961–62:

Sēfer Yᵉṣîrāh, the Hebrew edition with Ten Hebrew commentaries, reproduced by photo-offset, Sh. MWZNWN, Jerusalem.

Silva 1972:

Nicolau Duarte Silva, *Cabral e os Fenícios*, Edicão do Autro, São Paulo, Brasil. (Reprinted from *Revista do Arquivo Municipal*.)

Sepharial (no date):
>   The Book of Charms and Talismans, David McKay Company. Philadelphia.

Skelton-Marston-Painter 1965:
>   R. A. Skelton, Thomas E. Marston, George D. Painter, The Vinland Map and the Tartar Relation, Yale University Press, New Haven and London.

Stenring 1970:
>   Knut Stenring, The Book of Formation (= Sēfer Yᵉṣîrāh by Akiba ben Joseph), translated from the Hebrew with annotations, Ktav Publishing House, New York.

Sweet 1969:
>   R. F. G. Sweet, "A Pair of Double Acrostics in Akkadian," Orientalia, Volume 38, pp. 459–60.

Trillin 1972:
>   Calvin Trillin, "U.S. Journal: Maine—Runes," The New Yorker, 5 February 1972, pp. 70–74.

Van den Branden 1968:
>   A. Van den Branden, "L'inscription Phénicienne de Paraiba (Brésil)," Melto, Volume 4, pp. 55–73.

Wahlgren 1958:
>   Erik Wahlgren, The Kensington Stone: A Mystery Solved, University of Wisconsin Press, Madison, Wisconsin.

Washburn 1971:
>   Wilcomb E. Washburn (ed.), Proceedings of the Vinland Map Conference, University of Chicago Press, Chicago and London.

Wilson 1969:
>   Edmund Wilson, The Dead Sea Scrolls 1947–1969, Oxford University Press, New York.

Wright-Fowler 1971:
>   Louis B. Wright and Elaine W. Fowler, West and by North, Delacorte Press, New York.

Wuthenau 1969:
>   Alexander von Wuthenau, The Art of Terracotta Pottery in Pre-Columbian Central and South America, Crown Publishers, New York.

Wuthenau 1972:
>   Alexander von Wuthenau, "The Importance of Lambityeco," Revista, University of the Americas, Mexico, pp. 14–17.

Yadin 1969:
>   Yigael Yadin, Tefillin from Qumran, The Israel Exploration Society and the Shrine of the Book, Jerusalem, 1969.

Zitzer 1972:
>   Aurora Zitzer, "Further Developments in Diffusionism," Revista, University of the Americas, Mexico, pp. 10–13.

GLOSSARY

ABSOLUTE (STATE)

the term in Semitic linguistics applied to the form of nouns and adjectives when they stand by themselves, without a pronominal suffix or a following genitive

ACROSTIC

a message conveyed by reading down (vertically) the letters at (or near) the beginning of the lines of a composition; for example:

> Jokes
> About
> New
> Events

provides the name JANE acrostically.

ACROSTIC-TELESTIC

a message or messages conveyed simultaneously by reading down (vertically) the letters at (or near) the beginning and end of the lines of a composition; for example:

> JokeS
> About whoM
> Manfred and I
> Easily freT
> Sound harsH

yields JAMES as the acrostic and SMITH as the telestic.

ARAMEAN

pertaining to the speakers of the Northwest Semitic dialects known as Aramaic and Syriac

ARAMAIC

a Semitic language, belonging (along with Canaanite and Ugaritic) to the Northwest branch of the Semitic family

ASSEMBLAGE

a group of archaeological objects discovered together in a way that indicates they were in use at the same period

ASSYRIOLOGY

the study of ancient Mesopotamia (Iraq), with emphasis on the cuneiform inscriptions in Sumerian, Babylonian, and Assyrian

ATBASH

a Hebrew cipher whereby the first letter of the alphabet is replaced by the last letter of the alphabet, the second letter by next-to-the-last, and so forth

BABYLONIAN

the main branch of the Semitic language of ancient Mesopotamia (Iraq); it was written in cuneiform

BINDRUNE

two or more runes written as one sign through sharing a vertical line present in each of the individual runes

CANAANITE

the closely related dialects of Israel, ancient Lebanon, and some adjacent areas; they include Hebrew, Phoenician, Moabite, Edomite, etc.

CAVEAT EMPTOR

Latin for "let the buyer beware"

CIPHER

any system of transforming plaintext into a cryptogram, usually by substitution (of letters, not words) or transposition; to be distinguished from a code, where whole words or even phrases are replaced according to a code book in the form of a dictionary that lists the words of the plain language alphabetically, followed by their secret substitutes

COLOPHON

a notation added at the end of a text by the scribe

CUNEIFORM

any system of writing consisting of triangular wedges, with or without linear extensions

CRYPTANALYSIS

the solution of cryptograms without the help of keys, code books, or other aids; to be differentiated from cryptography

CRYPTOGRAM

a message in secret writing

CRYPTOGRAPHY

the composing of cryptograms, or their solution by use of keys, code books, or other aids; to be differentiated from cryptanalysis

DENDROLOGY

the scientific study of trees

COVER TEXT

a composition that makes plain sense, while concealing a cryptogram; thus "Down Old Nantucket They Will Always Interest Tom" is a cover text concealing the message "DON'T WAIT" as spelled out by the initial letters

DRAMATIS PERSONAE

Latin for "the persons of a drama" = "the cast"; may be used to designate the people involved in some development

ECUMENE

derived from the Greek *oikoumēnē*, "the inhabited world"; may be used in the sense of a large cultural continuum; for example, Europe and America have so much common background and interrelations that they may be regarded as parts of the same ecumene

ENCIPHERMENT

the concealment of meaning by substitution of letters or groups of letters, or by transposition

EPIGRAPHY

the study of inscriptions

ESOTERICA

things or subjects that are strange or unknown to most people

ESTABLISHMENT

the group of conformists in whom is vested the confidence of society; the particular group varies from subject to subject: thus the medical establishment is composed of conformist physicians (in the AMA in America, in the BMA in Britain, etc.), while the legal establishment is composed of conformist lawyers (in the American Bar Association)

ETHNOCENTRISM

an exaggerated concern with one's own ancestral background

GRAPHOLOGY

the study and analysis of individual handwriting

HAGIOGRAPHIC

pertaining to writings about saints or sacred matters

HELLENIST

an expert in Greek studies

INDICATOR

a feature that tells how to proceed in solving a cryptogram

IN SITU

Latin for "in place"; used of archaeological discoveries found in their original place; for example, an inscription found by excavators in the room of an ancient palace has been discovered "in situ," as opposed to a similar inscription found on sale in an antiquities shop

LEGEND

an inscription as on a map or coin

LEVANT

the East Mediterranean lands

LEXICAL

pertaining to vocabulary

LINGUISTICS

the scientific study of languages; to be differentiated from philology

MNEMONIC

any device to help us remember

MONOGRAM

two or more letters fused into one sign; runic monograms (excluding bindrunes which are quite common) occur so far only in Spirit Pond Runestone #3

NEOLITHIC

pertaining to the most refined of the Stone Ages, when men produced polished or well finished stone implements and other stone objects

NORDIC

used as a synonym of Scandinavian

NORSE

pertaining to the lands of the Scandinavians, particularly Norway; Old Norse designates the common language of the premodern Scandinavians

OBVERSE

the front side (as of an inscribed tablet or coin)

OTTOMAN

pertaining to Turkey under the Sultans whose regime gave way to the modern Turkish Republic after World War I

PALEOGRAPHY

the study of ancient writing, i.e., script (not literature)

PAX ACADEMICA

Latin for "the academic peace," in the sense of keeping the professors happy by not deviating drastically from generally accepted views

PENTATEUCH

the first five books of the Bible, known as the Books of Moses, or "The Law"; to wit, Genesis, Exodus, Leviticus, Numbers, and Deuteronomy

PENTATHIC NUMERALS

the old Nordic system of numerical signs, so called because "5" (*penta* in Greek) has a distinct form, deviating from the pattern of "1" to "4"

PER SE

Latin for "through itself," often used in the sense of "in itself"

PHILOLOGY

the study of written records

PHOENICIAN

any of the closely related Northwest Semitic dialects used by the ancient seapeople of Syria-Lebanon, embracing Tyre, Sidon, Byblos, Arwad, etc., or their colonies; in antiquity the Greeks used the term more broadly to include all Semitic merchant mariners with whom they came in contact

GLOSSARY 177

PHYLACTERIES
protective amulets; specifically a pair of little boxes containing Scriptural passages, attached by observant Jewish men, to their forehead and arm, by leather straps, during morning prayers except on Sabbath; they are called *tefillin* in Hebrew

PLAINTEXT
any document whose surface meaning makes sense, regardless of whether or not it conceals a cryptogram; the plaintext "George Owns Ninety One Walruses" conceals in its initial letters the cryptogram GO NOW

POLYPHONY
the attribution of more than one sound to a written symbol; thus the letter S is polyphonous in English with four different phonetic values as in: (1) see, (2) please, (3) sugar, and (4) pleasure

POST MORTEM
Latin for "after death"

PSEUDEPIGRAPHON
a document whose title or contents attributes it falsely to some author or epoch

REVERSE
the back side, as of an inscribed tablet or coin

RUNE
a letter in the script of the old Scandinavians

RUNESTONE
a stone on which runes have been carved

RUNOLOGY
the study of runes and of the inscriptions written in them

SECOND COMMONWEALTH
the Jewish community in Palestine during the centuries of the Second Temple (late sixth century B.C. to A.D. 70)

SIC
Latin for "so!"; used in brackets to indicate that the preceding word in a quotation is exactly as quoted in spite of an error—or something strange—in the original

SKERRY
a small rocky island

SOLECISM
a very unfamiliar feature or expression; an idiosyncrasy

STELA
a carved stone slab, often inscribed, to serve as a monument

SUBSTITUTION
any method of encipherment whereby an element is regularly replaced by some-

thing else; for instance, *a* is replaced by *b, b* by *c,* etc.; by this simple substitution cipher *dog* would be disguised as *eph*

TELESTIC

a message conveyed by reading down (vertically) the letters at (or near) the end of the lines of a composition; for example:

he haD
eaten A
buN

contains the name DAN as a telestic. The dictionaries prefer the spelling *telestich,* but since the last element (Greek *stich-*) is the same as in the more familiar *acrostic,* it is well to be consistent, especially in view of *acrostic-telestic.*

TRANSLITERATION

transposing anything written in one script into another system of writing; normally it consists of rendering a foreign script into Latin letters; it does not involve translation, which means rendering the sense in another language; for example, *day* is our transliteration of the Hebrew word that means "enough," whereas *day* is the English translation of the Hebrew word *yôm* which means "a day."

TRANSPOSITION

any cipher produced by rearranging the elements in the plaintext; for example, if each pair of letters are transposed, *cats* is enciphered as *acst*

UGARITIC

the language of ancient Ugarit: a Late Bronze Age port on the North Syrian coast; the language is Northwest Semitic, written in a cuneiform alphabet

VIZIER

a minister, especially a prime minister, in a Muslim country

VOX ASINORUM

Latin for "the voice of asses"

VOX DEI

Latin for "the voice of God"

VOX POPULI

Latin for "the voice of the people"

INDEX